BED and BREAKFAST: BREAKFAST: CALIFORNIA

D0040144

BED and BREAKFAST: CALIFORNIA

A Selective Guide

by Linda Kay Bristow

Illustrated by Linda Herman

CHRONICLE BOOKS   SAN FRANCISCO

LIBRARY OF CONGRESS CATALOGING IN
PUBLICATION DATA

Bristow, Linda Kay.
California bed and breakfast.
    1. Hotels, taverns, etc. — California—
Directories.
I.   Title.
TX907.B736   1982   647'.9479401
82-22086
ISBN 0-87701-196-6

BOOK AND COVER DESIGN
Linda Herman

COMPOSITION
Accent & Alphabet

PHOTO CREDITS
Page 9, courtesy of the Bed and Breakfast
Inn; page 15, courtesy of The Monte
Cristo; page 29, Patricia Bolfing; page 63,
Jim Beazley; page 65, courtesy of La
Residence Country Inn; page 67, Susan
Spann; page 75, courtesy of the Ink
House; page 79, courtesy of Chalet
Bernensis; page 81, courtesy of the
Chestelson House; page 99, courtesy of
the Elk Cove Inn; page 107, courtesy of
Glendeven; page 109, courtesy of the
Headlands Inn; page 111, courtesy of the
Joshua Grindle Inn; page 115, courtesy
of the Country Inn; page 135, courtesy of
the Mayfield House; pages 163 and 173,
Pat Hathaway.

Chronicle Books
870 Market Street
San Francisco,
California 94102

Table of Contents

Preface

When I began researching inns for *Bed and Breakfast: California* I was looking for places that fit my preconceived notion of what a bed and breakfast should be: a four- to six-guest-room home, owner occupied, at a reasonable price, breakfast inclusive. It didn't take long to realize that looking for the "definition-perfect" bed and breakfast was like looking for a needle in a haystack. Bed and breakfast inns come in all sizes, shapes, and price ranges. They vary greatly, due to factors such as locale, architectural style, and owner. And unlike their European counterparts, the American versions tend to offer an interesting alternative to the hotel/motel syndrome rather than an inexpensive night's lodging in someone's home.

Although much has already been written about the growing bed and breakfast trend, a guidebook is in order. There are now nearly 100 bed and breakfasts in California, and I hear of new ones all the time. In the following pages you'll find a review of eighty-eight such establishments in the state. Most are in areas of scenic or historic interest: the wine country, the Mendocino coast, the gold country, to name a few. Some are well known, others unknown. They are housed in buildings ranging in style from turn-of-the-century Queen Anne Victorians to former hunting lodges to newly built structures of concrete and glass. They contain as few as two rooms to as many as twenty. I have visited/stayed at almost all of them and have endeavored to give them a fair appraisal.

There is a certain etiquette involved with the bed and breakfast experience, and since forewarned is forearmed, here are some pointers to make you feel at home:

1. The basic modus operandi is the same as if you were staying at the home of a friend. Express appreciation for the offerings, be considerate, and don't treat the owner-innkeeper like a servant.

2. Don't hesitate to ask for what you want or need.

3. Clean up after yourself in a shared-bath situation.

4. Say goodbye when you check out, and return the key personally.

5. Follow house rules concerning check-out time, parking locations, payment arrangements, etc.

Some other points to remember: Rates are subject to change. (The rate structure I've used throughout the book can be interpreted as follows: inexpensive — under $50; moderate — $50 to $75; expensive — $75 plus.) Reservations are a must. (Though many inns book well in advance, last-minute cancellations do occur — don't hesitate to phone and ask.) A private bath is usually hard to come by. Don't expect a telephone, television, or room service. Smoking is discouraged, pets are unwelcome, and children are subject to house policy. Some inns require a two-day minimum stay, especially through weekend or holiday periods.

I enjoyed the inns, as I know you will, and I'd like to take this opportunity to extend my appreciation to the innkeepers throughout the state for putting me up as well as for putting up with me. A special thanks to the members of the Santa Barbara Innkeepers' Association for their many useful ideas and a taste of what the business is like from the innkeeper's side of the fence. Immeasurable gratitude to my dear friend and copy editor, Helga Wall.

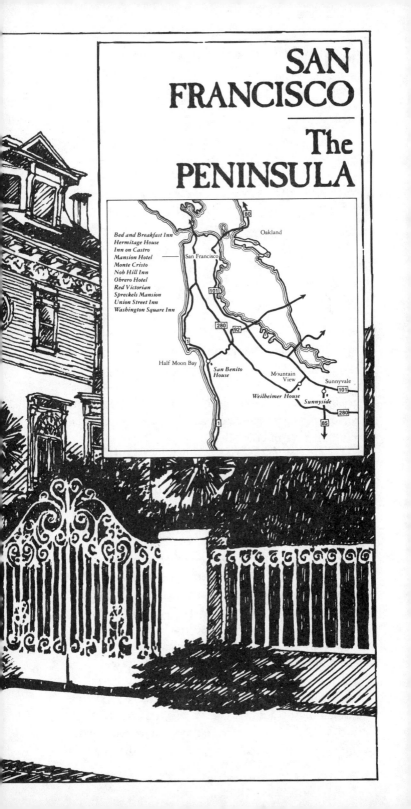

SAN FRANCISCO

The PENINSULA

Bed and Breakfast Inn
Hermitage House
Inn on Castro
Mansion Hotel
Monte Cristo
Nob Hill Inn
Obrero Hotel
Red Victorian
Spreckels Mansion
Union Street Inn
Washington Square Inn

Oakland

San Francisco

80

101

280

92

1

Half Moon Bay

San Benito House

Mountain View

Weilheimer House

Sunnyside

Sunnyvale

101

280

85

Spreckels Mansion

737 Buena Vista West
San Francisco, California 94117; (415) 861-3008

INNKEEPERS:	*Jonathan Shannon and Jeffrey Ross.*
ACCOMMODATIONS:	*Six rooms, four with private bath; queen-size beds.*
RESERVATIONS:	*Six weeks recommended.*
MINIMUM STAY:	*Two nights on weekends.*
DEPOSIT:	*First night's lodging.*
CREDIT CARDS:	*MC, VISA.*
RATES:	*Expensive.*
RESTRICTIONS:	*No children, pets, or cigar smoking.*

J onathan Shannon likes to think of the Spreckels Mansion as "a country inn in the city." And indeed he has a point. This elegant Victorian, built in 1887 for Richard Spreckels, sits high on a hill in a quiet neighborhood overlooking San Francisco's Buena Vista Park.

Of all the bed and breakfast inns I visited in San Francisco, this is one of my favorites. The atmosphere is comfortable, the rooms are spacious, the innkeepers are delightful, and there is plenty of parking (I mention this because in San Francisco parking space is a rare commodity).

Each room reflects the innkeepers' philosophy that "the room is as important a part of the traveler's experience as anything else." With the exception of the San Francisco suite, all the rooms are Victorian in feeling. Each is appointed with antiques, family treasures, and quality furniture. And each features an incredible view of the city. The San Francisco suite, which takes up the whole third story of the house, is decorated with contemporary furnishings and boasts a view of the city's skyline. The Sugar Baron suite is graced with tall fan windows, Corinthian columns, a pictorial-tile mantelpiece, and a canopied alcove that holds a queen-size bed. Its private bath is so enormous that you think you are walking into yet another suite. And what I wouldn't give for a soak in the freestanding tub in front of the fireplace just about now.

Breakfast at the Spreckels Mansion is light Continental: croissants, orange juice, and coffee or tea. In the evening guests (sometimes including United Nations ambassadors and Hollywood celebrities) mingle in the parlor to sip complimentary wine.

Nearby attractions include Haight Street shops and restaurants and Golden Gate Park. The inn is only fifteen minutes from downtown and the city's waterfront.

Hermitage House

2224 Sacramento Street
San Francisco, California 94115; (415) 921-5515

INNKEEPERS:	Dr. and Mrs. Frederick Binkley.
ACCOMMODATIONS:	Ten rooms, eight with private bath; twin, double, queen-, and king-size beds.
RESERVATIONS:	Three months recommended.
MINIMUM STAY:	One week.
DEPOSIT:	First and last night's lodging.
CREDIT CARDS:	MC, VISA.
RATES:	Inexpensive to moderate.
RESTRICTIONS:	Children discouraged. No pets.

Marian Binkley told me that for the past several years she has enjoyed "restoring old buildings on a shoestring." But as I toured the Hermitage House with her, I was quickly convinced that this lovely home was restored on much more than a shoestring (to say nothing of many hours of hard work). In fact, I remembered the building from the mid-seventies when it housed a drug rehabilitation center, and I could hardly believe the change.

This four-story Greek Revival was originally built for Judge Charles Slack sometime between 1900 and 1903. The Binkleys purchased the house in 1978 with the intent of turning it into rental units. But its ten bedrooms, seven working fireplaces, and spacious common areas made the house a natural for a bed and breakfast inn.

Two flights of stairs lead to the main entrance of the all-redwood house. Inside, the entryway shows off the beautiful carved heart redwood detail of the period in the pillars, beams, and stairway scrolls. High ceilings mark the first two main stories, and intricate inlaid designs are worked into the edging of the hardwood floors in the living room. A small alcove to the right of the entry was once used as a chapel for weddings and christenings.

Another flight of stairs leads to the bedrooms, the most impressive of which are Judge Slack's Study with its redwood shakes, beamed ceiling, bookshelf-lined walls, massive king-size bed, and view of the city; and the Master Bedroom with a king-size bed, a cozy sitting area in front of a fireplace, and a footed tub in its private bath.

The other natural that makes Hermitage House such a success as a bed and breakfast inn is Marion Binkley. She not only shows genuine interest in her guests, but her philosophy that "a bed and breakfast inn should be small, cozy, and homelike with a single (and stable) guiding force behind it" shines through.

Early risers will appreciate the ample breakfast, which is served buffet style in the downstairs breakfast room from 7:30 A.M. on. The fare consists of freshly squeezed orange juice, a selection of rolls with butter and jam, an assortment of hot and cold cereals, fruit, coffee, tea, and hot chocolate. Guests are free to take a tray to their room or out to the sun deck.

Hermitage House is one of only a few inns that allow (and even encourage) guests to make use of the kitchen facilities, which are conveniently set up for cooking and serving meals. The refrigerator can be used to store groceries, and all the other essentials (pans, dishes, and utensils) are on hand. This, along with private phones available on request and laundry and dry cleaning services, makes the Hermitage House more than just an inn. In fact, major corporations refer their favorite clients and top executives to the Hermitage.

The inn is located in the city's Pacific Heights district. The No. 1 California bus (which goes to the heart of the financial district) stops only a block away. The Fillmore and Union Street shopping areas are within walking distance, and Japantown is just a few blocks away.

Union Street Inn

2229 Union Street
San Francisco, California 94123; (415) 346-0424

INNKEEPER:	*Helen Stewart.*
ACCOMMODATIONS:	*Five rooms, two with private bath; double, queen-, and king-size beds.*
RESERVATIONS:	*Six weeks recommended.*
MINIMUM STAY:	*Two nights on weekends.*
DEPOSIT:	*First and last night's lodging.*
CREDIT CARDS:	*AE, MC, VISA.*
RATES:	*Moderate to expensive.*
RESTRICTIONS:	*Children: Minimum age 12. No pets.*

For Helen Stewart, owning and operating a bed and breakfast inn is a third career. As a mother she raised five children, and she has also taught school. As an innkeeper she is a natural. Helen's appealing calmness is reflected in the decor and surroundings of her Union Street Inn.

This two-story house, an Edwardian built around the turn of the century, is slightly set back from the bustle of Union Street. A few steps lead to a small front porch that opens to the reception area and downstairs parlor. The parlor, where guests gather in the late morning and early evening, has a soft apricot velvet wall covering, a brick fireplace, bay windows, and glass doors that open out to a back deck and garden. The furnishings, rich in tone and texture, are contemporary with a mix of antiques; the most unusual pieces are a pair of iron and brass chairs, with leather backs and seats, that were made in Australia. A bowl of potpourri made from the flowers in the garden sits on one of the end tables.

There are five bedrooms; two have a private bath and the other three share two bathrooms. Although the rooms range in price from $64–$94 per night, I found one to be just as nice as the next. Wildrose (one of the least expensive) has a persimmon-mauve decor and features a double brass bed, an abundance of healthy-looking green plants, and a garden view. The Golden Gate room, with a queen-size canopy bed in contrasting shades of midnight blue and mocha-cream, looks out to Union Street. To ease the "shared bath" situation there are sinks in every room, and bathrobes are provided.

The morning I spent at the Union Street Inn I relaxed on the sun deck with a glass of orange juice, a steaming hot cup of coffee, and one of the most delicious croissants I've ever tasted. Helen told me that she and her staff "taste-tested" just about every croissant made in San Francisco until they finally settled on one made at a French bakery a few blocks away. Between the breakfast, the morning sun, and the gentle breeze that filled my senses with the fragrance of the many varieties of flowers in the garden, I found it difficult to leave.

Those who can manage to tear themselves away from this peaceful and visually pleasant environment will find some of the city's finest shops and restaurants just a short distance from the door. Fisherman's Wharf, Pier 39, the new symphony center, the Opera House, and downtown San Francisco are minutes away.

The Bed and Breakfast Inn

Four Charlton Court
San Francisco, California 94123; (415) 921-9784

INNKEEPERS:	*Robert and Marily Kavanaugh.*
ACCOMMODATIONS:	*Eight rooms, four with private bath; twin, double, queen-, and king-sized beds.*
RESERVATIONS:	*Two to three months recommended.*
MINIMUM STAY:	*None.*
DEPOSIT:	*First night's lodging.*
CREDIT CARDS:	*Not accepted.*
RATES:	*Moderate to expensive.*
RESTRICTIONS:	*Children: Minimum age 12. No pets.*

The Bed and Breakfast Inn, opened in 1976, was the first b&b in San Francisco. Many have opened since, but this is still one of the most popular in the city, evidenced by comments like this one in the inn's guest book: "In my fifteen years of coming to San Francisco this was my favorite visit because of you."

At the time of the inn's opening, the owners, Robert and Marily Kavanaugh, didn't realize they had hit on an idea whose time had come. Having traveled extensively, they were anxious to open an inn patterned after those they had stayed at in Wales and Scotland. Bob's background in real estate and building and Marily's industriousness and flair for decorating led them to purchase and restore this one-hundred-year-old Victorian, which is located in a quiet cul-de-sac off fashionable Union Street that reminds one of a London mews.

Although today the Kavanaughs are assisted by a friendly staff of five, Marily explained that they did everything themselves for the first three years they were in business. I didn't find this hard to believe, as the afternoon I arrived I found her ironing table linens while Bob was busy with odd jobs in the garden.

It is apparent that the Kavanaughs take great pride

in what they do — and they do it well. On arrival, guests are greeted on a first-name basis and escorted to their room, where personal touches such as fresh flowers and fruit are evident.

Many of the rooms, such as the Mayfair, Covent Garden, and Kensington Gardens, are named after areas of London. Each room is unique in decor; antiques and family heirlooms are judiciously scattered throughout.

My favorite room is Celebration, one of the four available with a private bath. And what a bath — complete with a sunken double tub, a hand-painted Sherle Wagner pedestal basin, plush towels, and scented soaps and bath oil. The bedroom, papered with a blue and white Laura Ashley print, features a love seat and a queen-size bed. Another popular guest room (and one of the two that open to the garden) is the Willows, decorated in green and white print accented by white wicker furniture.

The Continental breakfast, served on Wedgewood china, includes fresh-squeezed orange juice, warm croissants, freshly ground coffee, and herbal tea. Evening sherry is complimentary, current magazines and good books are plentiful, and, unlike many other b&b inns, rooms with televisions and telephones are available.

The Bed and Breakfast Inn is located between Laguna and Buchanan in the heart of Union Street's sixteen blocks of boutiques, restaurants, and antique shops.

Inn on Castro

321 Castro Street
San Francisco, California 94114; (415) 861-0321

INNKEEPER:	*Joel Roman.*
ACCOMMODATIONS:	*Five rooms, all with shared bath; twin, large double, and king-size beds.*
RESERVATIONS:	*Four to six weeks recommended.*
MINIMUM STAY:	*Two nights.*
DEPOSIT:	*First night's lodging.*
CREDIT CARDS:	*MC, VISA.*
RATES:	*Moderate.*
RESTRICTIONS:	*No children. No pets.*

T he Inn on Castro, though housed in a 1910 Victorian (just up the hill from the intersection of Market and Castro streets), is strictly contemporary in interior design and furnishings. Although the mix of guests ranges from royalty to prim and proper elderly ladies, the inn caters primarily to a gay clientele.

The innkeeper (a native New Yorker) is Joel Roman, artist and interior designer. While attending the Academy of Fine Arts in Bologna, Italy, Roman traveled through Europe, staying at bed and breakfast inns. He determined then to open one of his own in San Francisco when he returned to the United States. His inn, opened in 1980, now serves as his personal art gallery, with his works enhancing the guest rooms, hallways, and common areas.

The inn has five guest rooms and 2½ shared baths. The rooms all sport Italian names. The striking features of Il Camino (the Fireplace) are its ornate brass bed, wicker chairs and baskets, abundance of thriving green plants, multicolored umbrella ceiling, and bay windows with vertical blinds. La Serra (the Greenhouse) has a window that looks out to a greenhouse directly off the bedroom. A private phone is available on request. A pay phone as well as a wet bar (refrigerator, sink, and ice maker) are located in the central hallway that runs the length of the building.

Common areas (which serve as showplaces for Roman's glass collection) include the upstairs living room, a gathering place for stimulating conversation and informal cocktails in the late afternoon; and the dining room, where breakfast is served. Breakfast starts at 8:30 A.M. with a glass of fresh fruit juice (usually orange or grapefruit), heavenly croissants from Delices de France (one of the city's well-known bakeries), butter and jams imported from London, and, of course, coffee and tea.

After breakfast you can wander around the Castro Street shops, see Mission Dolores, or take the bus to Haight Street or Golden Gate Park. Public transportation is plentiful.

Obrero Hotel

1208 Stockton Street
San Francisco, California 94133; (415) 986-9850

INNKEEPER:	*Bambi McDonald.*
ACCOMMODATIONS:	*Twelve rooms, all with shared baths; twin and double beds.*
RESERVATIONS:	*Two weeks recommended.*
MINIMUM STAY:	*Two nights.*
DEPOSIT:	*First and last night's lodging.*
CREDIT CARDS:	*Not accepted.*
RATES:	*Inexpensive.*
RESTRICTIONS:	*No pets. Quiet children are welcome.*

I would dub the Obrero Hotel the "no-frills bed and breakfast inn." But to use the words of the hotel's owner-innkeeper, Bambi McDonald, it is "a twelve-room (none of them perfect) European-style pension with an emphasis on cleanliness and value." And talk about value—this is certainly one of the least expensive places to stay in San Francisco (or anywhere, I might add), with prices ranging from $18 single to $34.50 triple occupancy.

But the Obrero is not for everyone, and it's not without its problems, as Bambi will be the first to admit. As a "for instance," the building's water heater only holds fifty gallons (I'll leave the rest to your imagination). But independent people interested in meeting similar types and in staying in the city at bargain prices find that the Obrero just fills the bill. A normal day at the hotel finds the gamut of visitors ranging from European students to bird-watchers from Bolinas, with a few filmmakers thrown in.

Because Ms. McDonald lived in Europe for several years and worked for friends who ran a pension in Amsterdam in exchange for room and board, she was not unfamiliar with the business. But striking out on her own in San Francisco wasn't as easy as she had imagined. It took three long, hard years to build up a reputation, and as she approaches her fourth year in business she still works seven days a week, twelve hours a day. In fact, she runs the whole operation with just one waitress, one maid, a strong dose of self-discipline, and a tight fist.

The hotel's twelve rooms share four baths, and the room furnishings are simple and sparse. Bambi describes a typical room as including "the best bed I could buy, a brass headboard, one chair, a dresser, a closet, and a sink with hot and cold running water."

Breakfast is served family style from 8:00 to 8:45 A.M., and it's enough to last through an entire day of sightseeing. A morning's sampling includes a four-minute egg, ham, cheese, an orange, hot sourdough bread, and tea and coffee — all included in the price of the room.

Family-style dinners featuring French Basque cuisine are served nightly. There are two entrées each night; sample fares include oxtail stew, cassoulet, Basque chicken, and shepherd's pie. Dinner comes with soup, salad, dessert, wine, and coffee — all for the bargain price of $7.50.

The hotel is conveniently located in the heart of San Francisco's Chinatown on the edge of North Beach, the Italian section of the city. Fisherman's Wharf and Union Square are just a stone's throw away.

The Monte Cristo

600 Presidio Avenue
San Francisco, California 94115; (415) 931-1875

INNKEEPER:	*Frances Young.*
ACCOMMODATIONS:	*Fourteen rooms, eight with private bath; twin, double, and queen-size beds.*
RESERVATIONS:	*Three to four weeks recommended.*
MINIMUM STAY:	*None.*
DEPOSIT:	*First night's lodging.*
CREDIT CARDS:	*AE, MC, VISA.*
RATES:	*Moderate to expensive.*
RESTRICTIONS:	*No pets.*

A couple from Laramie, Wyoming, described their stay at the Monte Cristo, one of San Francisco's newest bed and breakfast inns, as "a page from a storybook romance." And it's certain that the Monte Cristo has had many pages of romance throughout its history, as it was originally built as a hotel in 1875 and was well known as a bordello at various times.

All that aside, surely today the Monte Cristo is at the height of its glory, thanks to the efforts of the current innkeeper, Frances Young. Frances, a former nurse, a former Marinite, and a native of Winnipeg, Canada, is just the type you'd expect to find running an inn. She is a culturally sophisticated person who is anxious to please and is full of tidbits on current theater performances, gallery and museum exhibits, and the area's best restaurants. Because Frances lives on the premises, she feels that each individual is a guest in her home rather than just a paying client.

The Monte Cristo has been superbly restored. And once you enter your bedroom door, it can even be forgiven the long, somewhat dark hallways that run the length of the building. With few exceptions, the rooms are spacious. All are quite comfortable. Furnishings are Early American and English antiques, and each room has a large silk flower arrangement color-keyed to the wall-

paper. The rooms have various names and themes: the Violet Room, the Wicker Room, and, my favorite, the English Four-Poster Room, which is done in shades of blues, mauves, and beige.

The Chinese Wedding Bed Room has an elaborate and inviting teak bed with a down comforter. If you've never heard of a Chinese wedding bed, don't feel bad. Neither had I. A wedding gift to a bride from her parents, the wedding bed is handed down in the bride's family through the years, eventually becoming an heirloom. The wealthier the family, the more elaborate the bed. And from the looks of this one the family must have been the equivalent of America's Rockefellers. Chinese accents fill the rest of the room, and robes are provided for the trip down the hall to the shared bath.

The Monte Cristo is one of the few inns in the city that serve a full breakfast. Everything is home baked. The orange juice is freshly squeezed. The coffee cake comes straight from the oven. I left asking for the pancake recipe (what's so special about pancakes? — wait until you've tried these).

The Monte Cristo is located at the corner of Pine and Presidio, just a short walk from the Sacramento Street shops and restaurants. Major bus lines take you to Golden Gate Park, Fisherman's Wharf, or downtown in about fifteen minutes.

The Mansion Hotel

2220 Sacramento Street
San Francisco, California 94115; (415) 929-9444

INNKEEPER:	Robert Pritikin.
ACCOMMODATIONS:	Eighteen rooms, all but one with private bath; twin, double, and queen-size beds.
RESERVATIONS:	Two to three weeks recommended.
MINIMUM STAY:	None.
DEPOSIT:	First night's lodging.
CREDIT CARDS:	AE, MC, VISA.
RATES:	Moderate to expensive.
RESTRICTIONS:	No pets.

Robert Pritikin's Mansion Hotel is one of those places I run into every once in a while that straddles the thin line dividing an inn from a small hotel. But there are certain features that move me to include it here. First of all, it's housed in a grand, twin-turreted Queen Anne Victorian that was built by Utah State Senator Richard Chambers in 1887. Secondly, the innkeeper's colorful personality, wit, and varied background make for lively conversation. And finally, there is an ample breakfast served in-room each morning.

The hotel is billed as "being in the middle of everything — yet a million miles away." "Everything" includes the not-too-distant downtown, Fisherman's Wharf, and North Beach areas. The "million miles away" is actually just a step away from the front porch to the grand foyer, with its gigantic crystal chandelier and a mural depicting the romantic characters who inhabited the Mansion nearly a century ago.

To the right of the foyer is the Music Room, the setting for nightly classical concerts and weekend magic shows. The innkeeper ("America's foremost classical saw player") is your master of ceremonies. The piano here is said to have belonged to Claudia Chambers, the Mansion's legendary haunt. (Claudia's bad manners are attributed as the cause of a host of the hotel's problems and troubles. But the staff snickers at the story of the night she unhinged a door that fell on the head of a guest who was being difficult.)

Another room worth noting is the Billiard Room. Beside the antique billiard table you'll find a stained-glass nickelodeon-player piano pumping out the tunes of John Philip Sousa and Scott Joplin. A collection of beaded Victorian purses is displayed on the wall above an outsized "dollhouse" that was the original set from Edward Albee's New York Broadway production of *Tiny Alice*. The glass-fronted armoires hold memorabilia.

Guest rooms occupy the second and third floors of the building. A brass plaque on the door of each room identifies the historic personage to whom the room is dedicated, and the walls of the room are alive with murals describing the legend of that person's life. Your room may have a marble fireplace, or a private terrace, or a ceiling that slants to the floor, but I can guarantee that it will have some interesting accents (a tapestry, an old trunk, a lace shawl) and a painting of a pig. Though they seem to add to the fun, the paintings are not always appreciated. Guests frequently take them down and put them out in the hallway. In one of the rooms I toured with Pritikin the painting was not only down, it was turned to the wall.

Breakfast anyone? How does a French croissant, a wineglass full of orange juice with a strawberry on the side, a hard-cooked "Easter" egg (found under the tea-cup), and freshly ground coffee sound?

Tennis? LaFayette Park is just a block away. Sauna? There's one in-house. Afternoon sherry? It's complimentary. Dinner? The hotel has an intimate dining room that features $23 entrées that will knock your socks off. There's Chicken Bazoom, the Ten-Thousand-Dollar Steak, and the Twenty-three-Dollar Potato spiked with vodka and stuffed with cream cheese, mushrooms, and imported black caviar. Last but not least are the front and back gardens displaying a collection of Beniamino Bufano sculptures, the most prominent of which are two towering bronze figures of Saint Francis of Assisi, the patron saint of San Francisco.

The Red Victorian

1665 Haight Street
San Francisco, California 94117; (415) 864-1978

INNKEEPER:	*Sami Sunchild.*
ACCOMMODATIONS:	*Fifteen rooms, three with private bath; twin, double, queen- and king-size beds.*
RESERVATIONS:	*Two weeks recommended.*
MINIMUM STAY:	*None.*
DEPOSIT:	*First night's lodging.*
CREDIT CARDS:	*MC, VISA.*
RATES:	*Inexpensive to moderate.*
RESTRICTIONS:	*No children. Pets by arrangement.*

Sami Sunchild is an artist-in-residence innkeeper; the Red Victorian is the grandest of all her works. This colorful bed and breakfast, located in the heart of San Francisco's ever-evolving Haight-Ashbury district, is a favorite of creative types and "new age" thinkers. Psychologists and architects, futurists and poets come here from as near as a block away to as far as New Zealand and the Orient.

This turn-of-the-century building was originally constructed as a resort hotel in the country. Today it is hard to believe that this area was ever "in the country." The hotel faded into a home for alcoholics and then in the 1960s it was invaded by hippies.

Sami purchased the property in 1977 and began single-handedly restoring the place to its original splendor. Today Sami believes that part of what makes the Red Victorian what it is is what it's not. It's not downtown. It's not in a frequented tourist area. And it's not for those who want to get away from it all or to just be alone. It is conveniently located near Golden Gate Park and is on major bus lines to all parts of the city.

The inn's "pink parlor," with its pink carpet and walls and lace curtains with red velvet valances, is the setting for lively discussions and occasional seminars where locals and guests meet, exchange ideas, and make friends. There's a meditation room that, in Sami's words, "is so quiet you can hear the quiet." And Sami's "lines of thought" art gallery of calligraphic paintings dominates the second- and third-floor corridors.

The guest rooms (located off the long, narrow hallways that run the length of the building) are moderately priced. The least expensive is the Green Room, which overlooks Haight Street. The best room in the house is the Peacock Suite, which features an electric fireplace, a crystal chandelier, and a king-size bed. The rooms are all simply furnished. Handmade quilts, Haight Street memorabilia, and old photographs of the hotel accent each room.

A light Continental breakfast of croissants, coffee, tea, and orange juice is served from 8:00 A.M. to noon in the pink parlor.

Nob Hill Inn

1000 Pine Street
San Francisco, California 94109; (415) 673-6080

INNKEEPERS:	*Rick Henriksen and Jim Brennan.*
ACCOMMODATIONS:	*Eighteen rooms, fifteen with private bath; twin, double, and queen-size beds.*
RESERVATIONS:	*Two to three weeks recommended.*
MINIMUM STAY:	*None.*
DEPOSIT:	*First night's lodging.*
CREDIT CARDS:	*AE, MC, VISA.*
RATES:	*Moderate to expensive.*
RESTRICTIONS:	*No pets.*

T he Nob Hill Inn is billed as a "small luxury hotel" decorated in Early European style. This Edwardian building was originally constructed in 1907 as temporary housing for Nob Hill residents left homeless by the great earthquake and fire of the previous year. In the 1920s it became one of the city's small hotels, and in 1945 the renowned Sally Stanford acquired the building and used it as a part of her brothel. The building was a thirty-room boarding-house just prior to its acquisition and transformation into an inn by partners Rick Henriksen and Jim Brennan.

And what a transformation. A step through the front door is a step back in time. The focal point of the inn is the nineteenth-century French glass-cage elevator (surely one of a kind) that sits perched between the reception desk and the front parlor. The parlor's original tile-faced fireplace and Louis XV and XVI furnishings and decor bring to mind the grand houses of Europe.

There are six guest rooms each on the second, third, and fourth floors. Six of the rooms have working fireplaces, two feature four-poster beds, and all have antique furnishings, either brass or wooden beds, and claw-foot tubs in the bath. Some of the rooms have stained-glass windows, and most have lace curtains and color-coordinated fabrics and wall coverings. A Krön chocolate and a fresh flower are placed on each pillow when the beds are turned down at night. (Room No. 12 is said to be haunted. The ghost is reputed to be one of Sally Stanford's girls, who met her death the night her jealous husband discovered her supplementing their meager income.)

Brennan and Henriksen leave the inn in the capable hands of Colin Childs, a native of England trained in hotel management by Grand Metropolitan Hotels. Childs lists the inn's homelike feeling, limited number of rooms, and Nob Hill location with its easy access to downtown, the cable cars, dining, shopping and theater as reasons "the inn is *the* preferred place to stay."

Unusual comforts here include room service of beverages and light snacks, dry cleaning and laundering services, telephone and television on request, and a small wine cellar just off the reception hall that is stocked with California wines and champagnes.

Croissants, fresh fruit, freshly squeezed orange juice, Viennese-blend coffee, and English teas are served in the drawing room from 7:00 to 11:00 each morning, or at bedside on Victorian wicker trays. Tea in the parlor is served from 4:00 to 6:00 in the afternoon.

The Washington Square Inn

1660 Stockton Street
San Francisco, California 94133; (415) 981-4220

INNKEEPERS:	*Nan and Norm Rosenblatt.*
ACCOMMODATIONS:	*Fifteen rooms, ten with private bath; twin, double, queen- and king-size beds.*
RESERVATIONS:	*Six to eight weeks recommended.*
MINIMUM STAY:	*None.*
DEPOSIT:	*First night's lodging.*
CREDIT CARDS:	*AE, MC, VISA.*
RATES:	*Moderate to expensive.*
RESTRICTIONS:	*Children not encouraged. No pets.*

San Francisco's Nan and Norm Rosenblatt "got the bug" for a bed and breakfast inn of their own while traveling through Europe and staying at little inns along the way. Nan is an interior designer, Norm a financial wizard. Together they turned two dilapidated buildings that sat back to back into one fantastic inn: the Washington Square Inn.

A stay at the inn is so pleasant that it's tempting to stay in, especially if you have one of the three rooms that overlook the square. Although the rooms are individually decorated, a "European country" theme prevails. Furnishings are a well-balanced mix of antique and contemporary. The beds are all modern, but some have fabric canopies that blend with the soft floral-patterned drapes and bedspreads. Most rooms have a private bath and all have a telephone. Televisions are available on request. As in most of the other inns in this book, there are fresh flowers in every room.

Complimentary breakfast-in-bed runs to flaky croissants, freshly squeezed orange juice, coffee (Italian, of course), and herb tea. Or if you prefer to meet and mingle with the other guests, you can enjoy breakfast at the formal dining table in the reception lobby.

Though it may be tempting, don't linger over breakfast too long. Washington Square is in the heart of the city's colorful Italian district, which offers plenty to see and do. This area, called North Beach, is a favorite of locals and visitors alike for its specialty shops, bakeries, cafés, and nightclubs, all within a few blocks' radius.

And if that's not enough, the inn's concierge can arrange a car, theater tickets, a tour of the city, a picnic, or even a stenographer if you've come here to get down to business (heaven forbid). (Because the inn is midway between Fisherman's Wharf and the financial district, it appeals to tourists and business people alike.)

There's tea, homemade shortbread, and cucumber sandwiches from 3:00 to 6:00 P.M. Wine tasting is a complimentary Friday-afternoon affair.

Weilheimer House

938 Villa Street
Mountain View, California 94041; (415) 967-5201

INNKEEPERS:	*Karl and Kathy Meier.*
ACCOMMODATIONS:	*Two rooms with shared bath; double and queen-size beds.*
RESERVATIONS:	*Two weeks recommended.*
MINIMUM STAY:	*None.*
DEPOSIT:	*First night's lodging.*
CREDIT CARDS:	*MC, VISA.*
RATES:	*Moderate.*
RESTRICTIONS:	*No pets.*

T here are several things I like about Weilheimer House, Mountain View's first and (to my knowledge) only bed and breakfast inn. It's small — very small in fact, with only two guest rooms, a shared bath, and a parlor. Children are welcome. And the house offers people with business on the Peninsula a great alternative to the often lonely motel experience.

But what I like most about Weilheimer House is the innkeeper, Kathy Meier. Bed and breakfast and Kathy Meier just seem to go together. Kathy is personable and she enjoys meeting and serving her guests. Although she's worked in a real estate office and as a drapery seamstress, her favorite role has always been housewife and mother to her now eleven-year-old daughter. Kathy, daughter, and husband Karl (an electrician by trade) use the back part of the house as their living quarters, so they are always on hand to converse, recommend the best restaurants, or provide directions.

The house, a Victorian with an old-fashioned veranda, a high gambrel roof, slanted bay windows, and clapboard siding, is located on a quiet residential street a few blocks from downtown Mountain View. It was built in 1900 by Julius Weilheimer, one of the city's first downtown merchants; his store building, now a men's clothing store, still stands on the main street. This was also once home to U.S. Congressman Arthur Free, and for a time it housed a doctor's office.

The parlor and the bedrooms are predominately furnished with American and English antiques, most of which Kathy has collected over the years, some of which were purchased at auction. The bedroom in the front of the house features a gleaming brass bed covered by a soft comforter. The back bedroom, or "Green Room," as it's called, has a large oak bed with an ornate head and foot board, a Victorian chandelier, and an armoire. Both rooms share a bath, complete with a Victorian basin and claw-foot tub, as well as a shower for those who prefer modern convenience.

An ample breakfast is served in the dining room from 7:30 to 9:00 A.M. The menu for the day might include a fresh fruit salad, cinnamon coffee cake, grape-fruit or orange juice, and coffee and tea. The freshly baked pastries come from Kathy's favorite nearby bakery.

Other than the downtown shops and restaurants, area attractions include Marriott's Great America and Marine World. The San Francisco airport is just thirty minutes away.

Sunnyside

435 East McKinley Avenue
Sunnyvale, California 94086; (408) 736-3794

INNKEEPERS:	*Byrd and Phyllis Helligas.*
ACCOMMODATIONS:	*Two units, each with private bath; one double and one queen-size bed.*
RESERVATIONS:	*Two weeks recommended.*
MINIMUM STAY:	*None.*
DEPOSIT:	*None required.*
CREDIT CARDS:	*Not accepted.*
RATES:	*Moderate.*
RESTRICTIONS:	*No children. No pets.*

B yrd Helligas has worn a number of hats in his time. He was a Unitarian clergyman for thirteen years, he drove a delivery wagon, he once ran a political campaign, and he's worked in the food processing and tobacco industries. But the hat he wears now, and perhaps the hat he wears best, is that of innkeeper. Byrd is one of those people who can fascinate and entertain you at the same time with a million and one stories about a million and one things. And at Sunnyside, his "urban inn," there are at least that many things to talk about.

The inn, housed in a former potato chip factory, is a virtual museum of old and new junk that Helligas has rescued from the indifference of friends, city dumps, and other undisclosed sources. A turn-of-the-century, gas-fired candy cooker has been turned into a table. Discarded circuit boards from the Peninsula's thriving electronic firms cover the walls of one of the bathrooms. A soda ash firecart (of the type that was used to put out fires after San Francisco's 1906 quake) serves as a planter. The automatic stapler that was used to seal the factory's potato chip bags now sits as a piece of unusual sculpture on the front lawn.

There are two units, each with a private bath with an old-fashioned bathtub and shower, a television, and a telephone. The Reznor Room (named after the large industrial heater situated here) holds a queen-size bed (with an extra-firm mattress) built on an old Sears Roebuck display case. A down comforter "between the sheets" covers the bed. The room adjoins an atrium. The other unit, the Cottage, undoubtedly takes its name from the cottagelike feeling supplied by the beamed ceiling. It has a self-contained kitchen complete with pots and pans, dishes, and utensils. There's a double bed and an 1840s walnut and marble step dresser the Helligases call "the obscene queen."

Breakfast seems to be subject to the whims of the cook, but you have your choice of either a Continental or a full country breakfast whenever you'd like it within a reasonable time range. Mine consisted of a three-egg omelette, a banana, French bread with cream cheese and jam, coffee, and a glass of wine (well, I did get a rather late start).

Sunnyside is located within easy access of the major freeways (101 and 280). It's a twenty-minute drive from San Jose and about an hour from San Francisco. Sunnyvale's downtown shopping area is a short walk away.

San Benito House

356 Main Street
Half Moon Bay, California 94019; (415) 726-3425

INNKEEPER:	*Carol Regan.*
ACCOMMODATIONS:	*Eleven rooms, nine with private bath; double beds (one room with twin beds).*
RESERVATIONS:	*Three weeks recommended.*
MINIMUM STAY:	*None.*
DEPOSIT:	*First night's lodging.*
CREDIT CARDS:	*AE,MC,VISA.*
RATES:	*Inexpensive to moderate.*
RESTRICTIONS:	*No pets.*

I can't wait to get back to San Benito House. This two-story, light-blue building on a corner of Half Moon Bay's Main Street offers a romantic bed and breakfast getaway just thirty-five miles south of San Francisco. Carol Regan, part owner and chef-in-residence, oversees the whole operation, which consists of eleven guest rooms on the second floor, a downstairs restaurant that serves classic country cuisine, a Western-style saloon with "local color," and a garden deli-café.

The inn was originally built by Estanislaus Zabella at the turn of the century and was known as the Mosconi Hotel. In the 1930s it changed ownership and was renamed Domenic's. Regan and partners (one of whom is husband Ron Mikelsen, owner of the Half Moon Bay Nursery) purchased the hostelry in 1976 and began a "three-phase" restoration project. The final phase (just completed at the time of my visit) entailed the careful restoration of each guest room to include fixtures and furnishings of the period.

The rooms are small but cozy. The one I called home was painted a forest green accented with white trim. There was a white iron bed with a fluffy comforter and an antique dresser with a huge bouquet of daisies in a wicker basket. (It helps to have a husband in the flower

business.) Old photographs of the hotel and Half Moon Bay scenes added a touch of interest, and a profusion of red geraniums in the flower box just outside the window added a splash of color. An upstairs deck provided a place to sit and look out over the ocean, and the sauna (the only modern concession in the whole place) was heavenly.

The evening started off with complimentary drinks in the saloon (weekends only), followed by a superb dinner of *fettucine* with fresh *pesto,* a garden salad, and rack of lamb ($14.95). As if that wasn't enough, I couldn't resist one of the French pastries that San Benito House is so famous for, Le Montmorency, a very rich chocolate cake with apricots.

Even though I was still feeling slightly full from dinner the night before, I came down for breakfast. And I have to admit that I'm glad I did. There was a strong cup of Graffeo coffee, "fresh from the oven" whole-wheat bread with sweet butter and marmalade, and fresh fruit. Though breakfast is usually served in the dining room, it can be had out in the garden, or taken on a tray to the room for a leisurely breakfast in bed.

Half Moon Bay's Pacific Ocean setting offers un-crowded beaches and an outstanding tide pool area. There are hiking trails through a nearby redwood forest and several local wineries for touring. Whale watching, fishing, horseback riding, and bicycling are popular area activities.

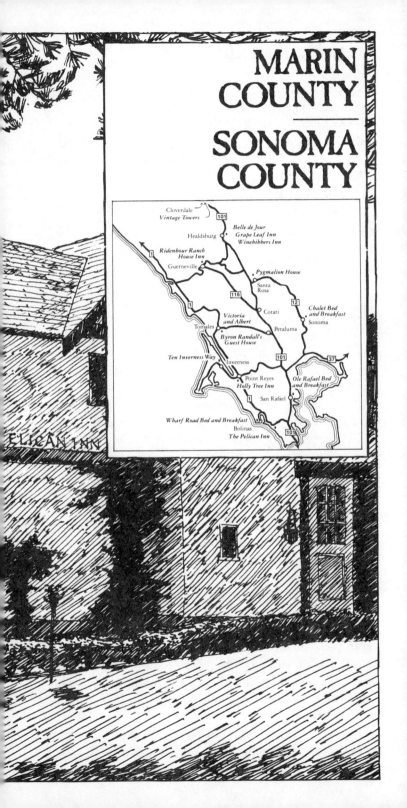

MARIN COUNTY — SONOMA COUNTY

Cloverdale
Vintage Towers

101

Belle de Jour
Grape Leaf Inn
Winehibbers Inn

Healdsburg

1

Ridenhour Ranch
House Inn

Guerneville

Pygmalion House

Santa
Rosa

116

Chalet Bed
and Breakfast

12

Cotati

Sonoma

1

Victoria
and Albert

Petaluma

Tomales

Byron Randall's
Guest House

Ten Inverness Way

101

37

Inverness

Point Reyes

Ole Rafael Bed
and Breakfast

Holly Tree Inn

1

San Rafael

Wharf Road Bed and Breakfast

Bolinas

101

The Pelican Inn

PELICAN INN

The Pelican Inn

10 Pacific Way
Muir Beach, California 94965; (415) 383-6000

INNKEEPERS:	*Charles and Brenda Felix.*
ACCOMMODATIONS:	*Six rooms, all with private bath; double beds.*
RESERVATIONS:	*Six months recommended.*
MINIMUM STAY:	*None.*
DEPOSIT:	*In full.*
CREDIT CARDS:	*AE, MC, VISA.*
RATES:	*Moderate.*
RESTRICTIONS:	*No pets.*

For bed and breakfast in the spirit of sixteenth-century England's west country, plan to stay at the Pelican Inn. The Pelican is located at Muir Beach, scarcely twenty minutes from the Golden Gate Bridge.

According to the innkeeper, Charles Felix, it was here on the Marin Coast that Sir Francis Drake beached his *Pelican* (the ship was renamed the *Golden Hinde* in mid-voyage) some four hundred years ago to claim California for Queen Elizabeth I and her descendants. Felix is not only a history buff, he's a fourth-generation publican of hearty British stock as well. In fact, he brought most of the Pelican Inn's furnishings and many of its superstitions from the family pub in Surrey.

The inn is a weathered-looking English Tudor-style farmhouse that sits nestled between the ocean and the redwoods of the Golden Gate National Recreation Area. The main floor of the building houses a traditional English pub and a public dining room. Pub grub includes meat pies, Scotch eggs, bangers, salads, home-baked bread, and desserts. The bar, with its low beams, dart board and good fellowship, is well stocked with imported brew (Bass, Watney, and John Courage on tap), wine, port, and sherry.

Overnight accommodations are located on the second floor. The rooms, with their low doorjambs and leaded windows, are graced with English antiques, heavily draped half-tester (canopy) beds, and Oriental rugs that cover the hardwood floors. Each room has a private bath. (Incidentally, the stone that hangs by a red silken thread over the bed is to insure that if conception occurs here the child will be born without rickets. "It's worked so far as I know," says Felix with a grin and a twinkle in his eye.)

Renaissance music, burning candles, and a roaring fire in the great inglenook set the tone for the proper English breakfast of bangers, bacon and eggs (any style), fried tomatoes, toast with Scotch marmalade, orange juice, coffee, and tea. The dashing white-haired Felix can be found mingling among the guests, chatting about topics ranging from his San Francisco advertising business to moustache wax.

A stay of any length is like an ongoing tea party. (And speaking of tea, Darjeeling tea with cakes and "all things nice" are served by the fire in the late afternoon.) You never know what's going to happen next. There are luncheon lectures, Elizabethan feasts, and Shakespearean excerpts on the front lawn.

Cricket anyone?

Holly Tree Inn

3 Silverhills Road
Point Reyes, California 94956; (415) 663-1554

INNKEEPERS:	*Diane and Tom Balogh.*
ACCOMMODATIONS:	*Four rooms, two with private bath; double and twin beds.*
RESERVATIONS:	*Four weeks recommended.*
MINIMUM STAY:	*None.*
DEPOSIT:	*In full.*
CREDIT CARDS:	*Not accepted.*
RATES:	*Moderate.*
RESTRICTIONS:	*No pets.*

Diane Balogh relates a story about the afternoon a young couple rode up on horses to inquire about a room for the night. But this was nothing unusual as the Baloghs' inn — the Holly Tree Inn — is located just a mile or so from Point Reyes National Seashore, which offers a variety of outdoor activities, among them hiking, fishing, boating, bird-watching, beachcombing, whale watching, and, of course, horseback riding.

This comfortable and spacious two-story home turned hunting lodge turned inn was built by a Swede in the late 1930s. The Baloghs, who had set their hearts on an inn of their own after staying at one in Maine in 1975, found the nineteen-acre estate on their first trip out with a realtor. They concluded the deal within a matter of days, moved in, and rented the downstairs as an apartment while the second-story conversion was taking shape. Opening day was July 14, 1979.

Central to the inn is the light, airy living room with its huge brick fireplace and overstuffed sofas upholstered in provincial prints. This is a wonderful place for conversation, a complimentary glass of wine in the afternoon, or a daydream or two.

The living room opens up to the dining area, which also features a fireplace and a cozy setting for the 9:00 A.M. buffet-style breakfast. One morning it might include waffles and sausage with fresh fruit, coffee, tea, and orange juice. The next you might get a sampling of Diane's quiche, or an omelette with homemade coffee cake or muffins.

There are only four guest rooms — the Laurel Room, the Holly Room, the Ivy Room, and the most recent addition, Mary's Garden — and I couldn't decide which I liked best. The Laurel Room is the most private as well as the largest. It is decorated in shades of pale blue and white, has a comfortable sitting area, and its twin-size beds can be adapted to a king. The lace-edged sheets and white ruffled curtains set the mood in the Ivy Room, with its view of the flowery hillside and ivied latticework just outside the cottage windows. The Holly Room over-looks the front lawn with its four well-manicured holly trees. Country antiques and peace and quiet are features the rooms have in common.

Unlike many other inns, the Holly Tree welcomes children. In fact the Baloghs have two very well-behaved children of their own.

Ten Inverness Way

10 Inverness Way
Inverness, California 94937; (415) 669-1648

INNKEEPERS:	Mary Davies and Stephen Kimball.
ACCOMMODATIONS:	Five rooms, all with shared bath; twin and double beds.
RESERVATIONS:	Four weeks recommended.
MINIMUM STAY:	None.
DEPOSIT:	$20.
CREDIT CARDS:	Not accepted.
RATES:	Inexpensive.
RESTRICTIONS:	No pets.

Ten Inverness Way is a five-bedroom, two-bath guest house that was built in 1904. The living room still has its original Douglas fir paneling and massive stone fireplace, and the guest rooms that were once family bedrooms retain that character. The entire house is furnished with what the proprietors call "comfortable antiques"; the rooms are filled with fresh flowers (daisies, fuchsias, carnations, and poppies, to name just a few) from the garden that surrounds the house.

Stephen Kimball (a real estate investor) and Mary Davies (a former Sacramento legislative analyst) are partners in the venture. Stephen backs the inn with money and muscle and Mary lends what can only be described as "the woman's touch": a feel for comfort, a flair for decorating, and a green thumb when it comes to gardening. Together, they've made Ten Inverness Way a "home away from home."

The living room is a great place to curl up with your favorite book. If you didn't bring one along you can choose from the wide selection that fills the bookshelf. The books (subjects range from religion to the arts, psychology to the classics) reflect the broad range of interests of the innkeepers. The player piano provides the evening's entertainment, and complimentary sherry can be enjoyed by the fire.

The bedrooms, all on the second floor, feature antique furniture, handmade rugs, and patchwork quilts. The most popular room in the house is at the top of the stairs. It's also the largest and the sunniest room; its four multipaned windows overlook the front garden.

There's a full American-style breakfast to start the day off right. Banana pancakes, quiche, and cheese-scrambled eggs are the specialties. Egg-based dishes might be complemented by homemade bread one morning or a freshly baked coffee cake the next. Fresh fruit, coffee, and tea come with every breakfast.

Ten Inverness Way is located just off Sir Francis Drake (the main street that runs through town). From the inn you can reach the village shops, restaurants, and Point Reyes National Seashore on foot. Golden Gate Transit provides service between San Francisco and Inverness; the bus stop is a block from the house.

Byron Randall's Guest House

25 Valley Street
Tomales, California 94971; (707) 878-9992

INNKEEPER:	*Byron Randall.*
ACCOMMODATIONS:	*Eight rooms, one with private bath; twin and double beds.*
RESERVATIONS:	*Two weeks recommended.*
MINIMUM STAY:	*None.*
DEPOSIT:	*Half the room cost.*
CREDIT CARDS:	*Not accepted.*
RATES:	*Inexpensive.*
RESTRICTIONS:	*No pets.*

I didn't see Byron Randall the entire time I was at his "famous Victorian Tomales guest house and art gallery." Neither did any of his other guests. It was rumored that he was in Seattle (or was it Vancouver?). No one seemed to know, no one seemed to care. The clientele (many of them "regulars") seemed to like Byron's laissez-faire way of doing business just fine.

Byron perfected his "absentee" system of inn-keeping after years in the business. (He is credited with opening the first guest house on the Mendocino coast some twenty years ago; he's been at the Tomales address for the past ten years.) The system, though confusing at first, is really quite simple: you sign yourself in, pick out the room you want, take the corresponding room key from a pegboard in the hall, and then make yourself right at home. Payment can be sent in advance, left on the way out, or forwarded at a time your conscience dictates.

The house, a redwood Victorian, was built in 1899. Oldtimers in the area (Swiss and Italian immigrants who settled here to develop the dairy business) refer to it as the "old Restano place," the showplace of its day. The size of the house makes it a natural as an inn. There are eight bedrooms. Each is furnished differently, but all the furnishings were salvaged from houses of the same time period. The upstairs rooms have beams and slanted ceilings as well as views of the garden. One of the downstairs rooms (with windows that face east to catch the morning sun) formerly served as Byron's studio. All the rooms display his paintings.

One of the weekend guests best described Byron's: "inexpensive (from $30), low key, and completely anonymous." A dozen or so other reasons to visit his guest house include the library, which is well stocked with books and games (there's also a fireplace and a piano), a fully equipped kitchen (its use is strongly encouraged), the outdoor patio, bullfrogs in the lily pond, white owls and chickens, blue jays and pathways, peace and quiet, and a friendly next-door neighbor. The house is two miles from Tomales Bay, ten minutes from Dillon Beach, and not far from the Russian River, Point Reyes National Seashore, and California's famed wine country.

Heretofore breakfast has consisted of strong coffee and "bring/cook your own." But in a telephone interview with Byron (yes, there really is a Byron) he informed me that he was instituting a light Continental breakfast: croissants with sweet butter and jam and fresh fruit to go along with the strong coffee.

I'll be checking back. Hope to meet you soon, Byron.

Victoria and Albert

Maine Street
Tomales, California 94971; (707) 878-2703

INNKEEPERS:	*Celeste McAdam and Evelyn Harper.*
ACCOMMODATIONS:	*Five rooms, all with shared bath; twin, double, and queen-size beds.*
RESERVATIONS:	*Three weeks recommended.*
MINIMUM STAY:	*None.*
DEPOSIT:	*None required.*
CREDIT CARDS:	*Not accepted.*
RATES:	*Inexpensive.*
RESTRICTIONS:	*No children. No large pets.*

Evelyn "Rusty" Harper and partner Celeste McAdam were looking for a bar business in Marin County until a realtor showed them a brace of houses (circa 1880) and coaxed them to "do something else." The "something else" they decided on was a b&b, and the two took up residence as innkeepers rather than saloonkeepers. The inn, Victoria and Albert, is located on Highway 1 in the small fishing village of Tomales. "Make no mistake," says Rusty, "we don't overlook the ocean. Our view is of the town post office and the general store."

Guest rooms are housed in Victoria, a two-story, peach-colored house. Breakfast is served in Albert the Wild West—era Victorian that Celeste and Rusty call home. Victoria's five rooms share two baths, a cozy parlor, and a small kitchen. Wine is set out in the parlor each evening. Kitchen privileges include use of the re-frigerator and stove. (An outdoor barbecue pit is also available for guest use.) Furnishings are a mix of old and new with emphasis on comfort rather than style. And the price is right: $35 for one of the most peaceful night's sleep I've had in a long time. The innkeepers sum up a Victoria and Albert experience in this way: "We're cheaper, we try harder, and we're a lot more fun." I concur.

On top of that they serve a breakfast that just won't quit. Mine began with a glass of orange juice followed by a bowl of just-picked raspberries (being an early riser I had the opportunity to watch Celeste pick them), two fresh eggs from the chicken coop out back, sausage patties, sautéed mushrooms and a slice of tomato, coffee, *and* a currant scone (recipe to follow). (The house specialty is said to be a homemade spinach and cottage cheese quiche — wish I could have stayed another day.)

Tomales (population 550 — sheep included, according to Rusty) is just a hop, skip, and a jump away from the Point Reyes National Seashore and Dillon Beach, and thirty-five minutes from the Russian River. As for me, the next time I go back I'm going to take along a good book and settle in.

Here's that recipe. *Currant Scones:* Mix together 3½ cups flour, 5 tsp. baking powder, 1 tsp. salt, and 4 tbsp. sugar. Using a pastry blender, blend in ¾ cup butter. Add 4 eggs, ½ cup milk, and ½ cup currants and mix well. Turn the dough onto a lightly floured surface and roll to ¾ inch thick. Cut the rolled dough into 4-inch squares; then cut each square into two triangles. Brush the tops with beaten egg yolk and sprinkle with sugar. Set 2 inches apart on a greased cookie sheet. Bake 10 – 15 minutes at 425 degrees. Makes 10 – 12 scones.

Enjoy.

Wharf Road Bed and Breakfast

11 Wharf Road
Bolinas, California 94924; (415) 868-0681

INNKEEPERS:	*Ashley and Stephen Ratcliffe.*
ACCOMMODATIONS:	*Two rooms, both with private bath; double and queen-size beds.*
RESERVATIONS:	*Two weeks recommended.*
MINIMUM STAY:	*None.*
DEPOSIT:	*First night's lodging.*
CREDIT CARDS:	*Not accepted.*
RATES:	*Inexpensive.*
RESTRICTIONS:	*Children: Minimum age eight. Pets discouraged.*

There are no road signs to Bolinas. Even though it is a unique town that nearly everyone finds charming, with wonderful beaches; an occasional art show, concert, or reading; and an interesting local bar, it has somehow managed to escape the mainstream. If you happen to be looking for Bolinas, however, you'll find it just off Highway 1 north of Stinson Beach. And once you find Bolinas, you'll easily find the newly opened Wharf Road Bed and Breakfast inn and Wild Rose Cafe. The two are neatly housed in one building — the second building on the left as you proceed north through town.

The enterprise is somewhat of a dream come true for Ashley and Stephen Ratcliffe, a young couple with a vision (and a friend in the business). They purchased the building at 11 Wharf Road early in 1981. Ashley claims responsibility for much of the renovation and the interior design. Additionally she is a fine photographer and a wonderful cook. Stephen holds a Ph.D. in English from U.C. Berkeley and makes his living as a writer and teacher.

The building, a small Victorian that predates the 1906 earthquake, is bordered by a sidewalk picket fence, a lovely rose garden, and a hillside of flowers and native shrubs. During the 1920s and 30s it was known as the

Adams Hotel, and in later years it was used as a single-family residence, an antique-print shop, a coffeehouse and a café. Ashley describes the renovation as "a big job, literally from the ground up — a new foundation, flooring, plumbing, wiring, and paint inside and out."

The overnight accommodations are reached by a flight of back stairs that lead to a private deck, a great place to sit with a cup of coffee and the morning paper. The clean white design of the rooms (white floors, white walls) suggests something of the tropics. There are natural-fiber rugs in the rooms as well as in the hall, a few antiques (claw-foot tubs with brass fittings, pedestal basins, iron beds), comfortable "mourri" chairs, some chintz, museum prints, and firm mattresses. Each room has a private bath.

Breakfast is on what I would call "the optional plan." You can choose to have breakfast included in the price of the room (the $45 plan). In this case you will be served coffee, freshly squeezed orange juice, and a homemade roll or popover in the downstairs café. Or you might be interested in ordering one of the delicious breakfasts on the menu at the Wild Rose; omelettes and pancakes with ham or bacon are the specialties. A third alternative is the Bolinas Bay Bakery (famous in Marin County for its croissants and cinnamon rolls) next door. Options No. 2 and No. 3 reduce the price of your room to $40 per night.

If you decide to give Wharf Road a try, be prepared. There are no road signs to Bolinas!

Ole Rafael Bed and Breakfast

1629 Fifth Avenue
San Rafael, California 94901; (415) 453-0414

INNKEEPER:	*Pat O'Shea.*
ACCOMMODATIONS:	*Five rooms, two with private bath; twin, double, and queen-size beds.*
RESERVATIONS:	*Two weeks recommended.*
MINIMUM STAY:	*None.*
DEPOSIT:	*$20 per night.*
CREDIT CARDS:	*Not accepted.*
RATES:	*Inexpensive.*
RESTRICTIONS:	*No infants. Pets discouraged.*

A ccording to the local historical society there was once a duel fought on the front lawn of the Ole Rafael Bed and Breakfast inn. Other than that, the owner and full-time innkeeper Pat O'Shea doesn't know too much about the house, except that it was built by an electrician named Klein in 1865 and that it is registered as one of California's historical homes.

Ole Rafael is one of a rash of newly opened b&b's in the state. Although it's not in the heart of any recognized tourist area, it's central to many: San Francisco, the Napa and Sonoma wine country, the Marin coastline, and the Russian River. From the inn it's an easy walk to downtown San Rafael and Mission San Rafael Archangel.

The house itself, which sits on a quiet, tree-lined avenue, is a two-story Victorian with a gabled front and a large porch (a fine place to relax on a warm Marin County afternoon). The spacious interior is due in part to the high ceilings. There are three fireplaces. A lovely spiral staircase leads to two of the five antique-filled bedrooms. The other three guest rooms are downstairs. One of them was once a sun porch that has been remodeled and expanded. Another room features an old-fashioned pot-bellied stove.

The innkeeper is a native Californian. While traveling through England she discovered bed and breakfasts and stayed at several such places. She enjoyed the comforts and hospitality offered by the hosts so much that she was inspired to open a bed and breakfast in her own home town. Although Pat hasn't been in the business very long, she already has a "most memorable experience" under her belt. Late one night a cute and (in her words) "very straight-laced looking" couple in their late forties knocked on her door and asked if she would take a picture of them in bed together. "She was in her nightgown and he in his pajamas," says Pat, "so I didn't see anything I wasn't supposed to."

Pat takes special pride in the home-cooked breakfast that she prepares for her overnight guests. She continually searches out new recipes and bakes all of the various breads, muffins, and other pastries that she serves along with a creatively prepared plate of fresh fruit in season. Special egg dishes are served at the whim of the cook, usually on the weekends. Cold cereal is always available for children (this is one of only a handful of inns that take children). Breakfast is served in the dining room at any hour within reason; the menu varies daily.

The Ole Rafael is accessible to Highway 101.

Chalet Bed and Breakfast

18935 - 5th Street West
Sonoma, California 95476; (707) 996-0190

INNKEEPERS:	*Patrick and Lolita Murphy.*
ACCOMMODATIONS:	*Four rooms share two baths; double beds.*
RESERVATIONS:	*Three weeks recommended.*
MINIMUM STAY:	*None.*
DEPOSIT:	*$15.*
CREDIT CARDS:	*Not accepted.*
RATES:	*Inexpensive.*
RESTRICTIONS:	*No pets.*

It was late when I pulled into Sonoma. "The Murphys have probably given up on me by now," I thought to myself as I fumbled around for the street map. At just about the same moment I crossed Fifth Street, but there was no sign of the Chalet — or anything resembling a bed and breakfast inn. I pulled the establishment's card out of my purse. " . . . overnite accommodations in a wonderful country farm setting . . . " Fifth Street didn't look like a "country farm setting" to me. I saw trailer courts and tract houses, gas stations and shopping centers, but no sign of "the country." Exasperated, I pulled up to a pay phone in Safeway's parking lot. "Hello, Lolita? H-E-L-P!"

All's well that ends well, so they say. And let me be the first to tell you that Fifth Street ends well — well up a one-lane dirt road. And yes, the Chalet, Sonoma's only bed and breakfast, is situated in a countrylike setting, complete with chickens and goats.

The house is a two-story Swiss chalet built in 1940. It is furnished with a mix of country antiques and collectibles: 1920 radios, patchwork quilts, wicker furniture, cast-iron stoves, Navajo rugs, an antique doll collection, and California pottery.

Accommodations consist of two downstairs bedrooms that share a bath and a sitting room, and two upstairs rooms with a shared bath. The upstairs parlor has a wood-burning stove and limited kitchen facilities. There's an extra bed for a child or a third adult in one of the downstairs rooms. The overall feel reflects Lolita's personal preference for "antiques, comfort, and good food."

Speaking of good food, the innkeepers offer a hearty, farm-style breakfast that starts off with freshly squeezed orange juice, a fruit cup, sausage and eggs (or the "omelette of the day"), a home-baked walnut coffee cake, and French-roast coffee. Fresh fruits and vegetables from the garden and eggs from the chickens are on the menu.

The Chalet is located in the Valley of the Moon, a fascinating area steeped in early California history and surrounded by wineries and vineyards. Sonoma's central plaza (a great place to sightsee, shop, and picnic) is just three quarters of a mile from the inn. The town bakery, a cheese factory, and a sausage shop supply all the makings for a picnic on the square or at nearby Jack London State Park.

Pygmalion House

331 Orange Street
Santa Rosa, California 95401; (707) 526-3407

INNKEEPERS:	*Maggie Kelly, Mike Geisler, and Jean Raible.*
ACCOMMODATIONS:	*Three rooms, all with shared bath; double beds.*
RESERVATIONS:	*Two weeks recommended.*
MINIMUM STAY:	*None.*
DEPOSIT:	*First night's lodging.*
CREDIT CARDS:	*Not accepted.*
RATES:	*Inexpensive.*
RESTRICTIONS:	*No pets.*

Santa Rosa was never on my "top ten" list of places to visit in California. But since I was searching out bed and breakfast inns and had heard that one had recently opened there, I thought I'd stop by. I spotted a beautifully restored (and freshly painted) Victorian from the freeway and something (perhaps intuition, perhaps experience) told me that if there was a b&b in Santa Rosa this was it. I followed directions a friend had jotted down: Downtown exit from 101. Third Street to Wilson. Left turn. One block to Hazel. Another left. A right onto Orange. Last house on the right. It came as no surprise that the last house on the right and the house I saw from the freeway were one and the same: Pygmalion House.

The house is a classic example of what one expects of a bed and breakfast. It has charm and history. It's furnished with Victorian antiques. And, from a typical bed and breakfast enthusiast's point of view, it's just the right size.

Three bedrooms share a bath and a half. Each room is named for the predominant color of its decor. The Blue Room wins my vote of approval: blue and white flowered wallpaper, plush blue carpeting, white wicker furniture, lace curtains, and a Bavarian iron bed with touches of brass and porcelain. The bathroom has an old-fashioned claw-foot tub with brass fixtures.

Guests enjoy a full breakfast brought to the room. A sample menu: a three-egg omelette, potatoes, hot rolls, fresh fruit in season, coffee, and juice. Other amenities: the morning paper, fresh flowers in the room, and brandy in the parlor in the afternoon.

Maggie Kelly, Mike Geisler, and Jean Raible take turns at playing innkeeper. The three are old friends who originally purchased the house as an investment, but decided not to sell when Maggie suggested it be used as a hostelry.

Pygmalion House is adjacent to Railroad Square, the historical part of Santa Rosa that is rapidly gaining popularity for its shops and fine restaurants. And (as I discovered) Santa Rosa is central to many areas of interest: the Napa and Sonoma wine country, the Russian River, San Francisco, Point Reyes National Seashore, and the ocean.

Ridenhour Ranch House Inn

12850 River Road
Guerneville, California 95446; (707) 887-1033

INNKEEPERS:	*Bob and Martha Satterthwaite.*
ACCOMMODATIONS:	*Five rooms, two with private bath; twin, double, and queen-size beds.*
RESERVATIONS:	*Four weeks recommended.*
MINIMUM STAY:	*Two nights on holidays and through the summer (June 15 to September 15).*
DEPOSIT:	*First night's lodging.*
CREDIT CARDS:	*MC, VISA.*
RATES:	*Moderate.*
RESTRICTIONS:	*Children: Minimum age ten. No pets.*

L ouis William Ridenhour was a homesteader from Missouri who came to California in 1850 and in 1856 began to farm the Ridenhour Ranch — 940 acres on both sides of the Russian River. In 1906 his son, Louis E. Ridenhour, constructed a handsome ranch house of heart redwood on 2¼ acres of the property. The younger Ridenhour's daughter Virginia, and her husband, former Assistant Surgeon General Justin K. Fuller, eventually came into possession of the house, and in 1954 they enlarged and improved it.

Martha and Bob Satterthwaite purchased the home in 1977 and worked for two years remodeling it into a bed and breakfast inn patterned after those they had discovered on trips through the eastern part of the United States. The result, Ridenhour Ranch House Inn, is one of the finest inns this side of the eastern seaboard.

This two-story, eleven-room house has five bedrooms, a large country kitchen, and a formal dining room. The comfortable living room beckons guests to relax, chat, read, play cards, put together a puzzle, or just sit and sip a glass of wine in front of the brick fireplace.

Each bedroom is individually and tastefully appointed with country English and American antique furnishings, quilts, oriental rugs, the finest-quality linens, flowers, and plants. The bathroom medicine cabinets are stocked with toothpaste, Band-Aids, and other essentials one might have left behind.

A complimentary breakfast of freshly ground coffee, juice, hot rolls and nut breads, fruit, and cheese is served each morning in the kitchen or the dining room. Trays are available for guests to take breakfast back to their room or out to the patio.

The informally landscaped grounds invite a stroll under the redwoods and oaks. The trees of the orchard yield a variety of fruit (apples, peaches, pears, and apricots) for picking and eating. A hot tub is available for guests' use. Secluded river beaches are a short walk away. One can walk to Korbel Winery for a tour of their champagne cellars.

A few things to note: (1) Rates are discounted 20 percent Sunday through Thursday, October to June (holidays excluded); (2) the inn is closed to the public during the months of December and January; (3) special arrangements can be made for group visits (the inn is an ideal spot for seminars).

Grape Leaf Inn

539 Johnson Street
Healdsburg, California 95448; (707) 433-8140

INNKEEPER:	*Laura Salo.*
ACCOMMODATIONS:	*Four rooms share two baths; double, twin, and king-size beds.*
RESERVATIONS:	*Three weeks recommended.*
MINIMUM STAY:	*None.*
DEPOSIT:	*First night's lodging.*
CREDIT CARDS:	*MC, VISA.*
RATES:	*Moderate.*
RESTRICTIONS:	*No children. No pets.*

T he Grape Leaf Inn, located in the small town of Healdsburg, is a short bicycle ride from one of California's premier grape-growing regions: Alexander Valley.

In keeping with the natural surroundings, innkeeper Laura Salo has furnished this restored Victorian to reflect the turn of the century and has named the four guest rooms after grape varietals. Cabernet Sauvignon has a double bed and an adjacent bath. The Chardonnay Suite features a private bath and a king-size bed. Sauvignon Blanc's brass and iron bed faces a bay window with a love seat. And the Zinfandel Room has twin beds, an armoire, and an Oriental rug that covers the hardwood floor.

Laura pours a sampling of Sonoma County wine in the front parlor late each afternoon. Books, magazines, and games are available, or one can just sit and relax on the custom-made sofa in front of the fireplace. A collection of local artists' paintings and photographs are on display throughout the inn.

Breakfast, consisting of freshly ground coffee, a glass of champagne, fruit and cheese, and freshly baked croissants and other delicacies, is served on fine china in the dining room. If guests wish they may choose to partake in the breakfast nook or on the veranda.

French pastry and coffee are set out in the evening.

The refrigerator is stocked with Sonoma County wine; guests are welcome to help themselves as well as to take full advantage of the kitchen facilities.

Within walking distance of the inn are night-lighted tennis courts and river beaches. Bicycles are available to guests of the inn for informal tours of the wine country. The innkeeper will make dinner reservations or arrangements for river canoe trips and other recreational activities.

Room rates are discounted 20 percent mid-week from November to March.

Winebibbers Inn

603 Monte Vista
Healdsburg, California 95448; (707) 433-3019

INNKEEPERS:	Jayne and Don Headley.
ACCOMMODATIONS:	Seven rooms, three with private bath; twin, double, queen-, and king-size beds.
RESERVATIONS:	Two to four weeks recommended.
MINIMUM STAY:	None.
DEPOSIT:	First night's lodging.
CREDIT CARDS:	MC, VISA.
RATES:	Moderate
RESTRICTIONS:	Children discouraged. No pets.

The People: Don and Jayne Headley, transplanted midwesterners who began buying and restoring Victorian mansions in San Francisco until they "tired of big-city problems and big-city politics" and began searching for . . .

The Place: Winebibbers Inn, two charming old homes tucked away on a hillside overlooking Healdsburg, in the heart of the Sonoma wine country.

The houses, as well as the rooms within them, are named for wineries along the Russian River Wine Road. The main house, referred to as the Landmark House, contains the community living room and breakfast area; the bedrooms honor Simi Winery, Johnson's of Alexander Valley, Sonoma Vineyards, and Dry Creek Vineyard. Guest quarters in the adjacent Foppiano House salute Geyser Peak Winery, Souverain Cellars, and Hop Kiln Winery.

Wine and earth tones set the decor throughout. Furnishings are a mix of contemporary pieces blended harmoniously with French, Dutch, and Scottish antiques. Antique prints and original works of art fill the rooms. The original bronze etchings are works of Jayne's uncle, Chester Lawson; paintings by Cameron Conrad grace the fireplace wall of the living room; and a group of sketches by Oakland's Rudy Tapiro depicts some of the Victorians restored by the Headleys over the years.

Guests rise to a breakfast that begins with an eye-opening cup of freshly ground coffee, a bowl of cold cereal complemented by the "fresh fruit of the day," and a slice of Jayne's home-baked pumpkin (or banana-nut) bread with sweet butter and homemade jam.

The inn's lush lawns invite sunny-day picnics, and the patio offers barbecue facilities for guest use. Ten-speed bicycles are available, tennis courts are nearby, the golf course is half a mile away, and (of course) nearby Russian River offers a day's worth of activities.

Belle de Jour

16276 Healdsburg Avenue
Healdsburg, California 95448; (707) 433-7892

INNKEEPER:	*Custis Piper.*
ACCOMMODATIONS:	*Four rooms, one with private bath; twin, double, queen-, and king-size beds.*
RESERVATIONS:	*Two weeks recommended.*
MINIMUM STAY:	*None.*
DEPOSIT:	*$35.*
CREDIT CARDS:	*AE, MC, VISA.*
RATES:	*Moderate.*
RESTRICTIONS:	*No children. No pets.*

When Custis Piper visits an inn there are three questions she asks: What's it like? What's to eat? And what's to do? Custis not only frequents inns, she owns and operates one: Belle de Jour, one of the three bed and breakfasts located in the wine country town of Healdsburg.

A visitor to *her* inn would have little difficulty answering the first of these three questions. What's it like? Exactly like a weekend visit to a farm, replete with goats, chickens, rabbits, and sheep. The farmhouse — a Victorian that was built sometime around 1875 — sits among six acres of fruit-bearing trees (pear, plum, and prune, to name a few). The atmosphere is informal, and as this is Ms. Piper's home as well as her single-handed commercial enterprise, the furnishings suit her taste. Included are Tiffany lamps and Victorian antiques, as well as antiques of other periods. The dining room features a fireplace, the living room a piano. Guest quarters include a large bedroom with a queen-size bed, a small room with a double bed (these rooms share the hall bath), and a double with a king-size bed and a private bath. For those with a real spirit of adventure, the recently remodeled bunkhouse (with a kitchenette and a half bath) accommodates three overnight guests.

What's to eat? The emphasis is on home-grown,

farm-fresh foods. Incorporated into the day's menu are fresh fruits, home-baked coffee cakes and croissants, fresh butter, eggs, and milk.

What's to do? That depends on your taste — and your energy level. The number one preference among the regular clientele is "absolutely nothing." For the more ambitious, field trips, tours of local wineries, bicycle tours, and picnics (a basket lunch is provided for a slight charge with advance notice) are all possibilities. There's the porch swing and (according to Custis) plenty of weeds that need pulling around the place.

Belle de Jour is open Wednesday through Sunday by reservation only. From Highway 101 take the Dry Creek Road off ramp. Turn right on Dry Creek to the stoplight; left on Healdsburg Avenue and continue for approximately one mile. The Simi Winery tasting room is on the left, Belle de Jour on the right.

Vintage Towers

302 North Main Street
Cloverdale, California 95425; (707) 894-4535

INNKEEPERS:	*Tom and Judy Haworth.*
ACCOMMODATIONS:	*Five rooms, one with private bath; double and king-size beds.*
RESERVATIONS:	*Three weeks recommended.*
MINIMUM STAY:	*None.*
DEPOSIT:	*$20.*
CREDIT CARDS:	*MC, VISA.*
RATES:	*Inexpensive.*
RESTRICTIONS:	*Children: Minimum age ten. No pets.*

L onging for the days when sitting on the porch swing with a glass of ice-cold lemonade was considered part of the American way of life? Wishing you could get away to a small town with a pace far removed from that of the city? Well, there's Vintage Towers, a grand Queen Anne Victorian located just a block east of Highway 101 in the town of Cloverdale.

This twenty-room mansion (built at the turn of the century by Simon Pinshcower, a wealthy Cloverdale merchant who aspired to own the biggest house in town) is owned and operated as a bed and breakfast inn by Tom and Judy Haworth. This hard-working but fun-loving couple managed to turn the house into the town's showplace as well as its showpiece.

The house has three working fireplaces, a library with over one thousand volumes, and a music room with a player piano, all for the guests' enjoyment. The five bedrooms (each architecturally unusual) are furnished with period pieces and named after their individual decor and theme; there's Scarlet's Room, Bordello Burgundy, the Calico Tower (three of the accommodations are tower suites), and the Circus Room, complete with a carousel and circus posters.

The Haworths' individual traits and talents are part of the attraction. Tom has a knack for making people feel right at home (he's from a family of nine!), and Judy (a home economics major) is a whiz in the kitchen. Her weekday breakfasts are simple but delicious: fresh fruit compote, homemade nut breads and muffins, and orange juice and coffee. Although I didn't sample the weekend menu first-hand, it's said to be a bit more substantial; Sunday brunch features entrées ranging from soufflés to eggs Benedict.

Cloverdale, a quiet New England—like town, affords one the pleasure of strolling past old houses and stately churches on tree-lined streets. Within minutes of the inn are many wineries, including Italian Swiss Colony. Secluded beaches and hiking trails are nearby. A half-day excursion might include a visit to the world-renowned geysers; a day-long journey begins down the Russian River Wine Road that starts in Cloverdale and goes all the way to Korbel Champagne Cellars near Guerneville.

Vintage Towers provides bicycles; canoes can be reserved locally. The Haworths own a twenty-five-foot sailing sloop that can be reserved for an afternoon on the nearby lake, and Tom can arrange an action-packed tubing trip down the Russian River.

Note: Accommodations are seasonal — March through October. Group reservations taken during winter months on request.

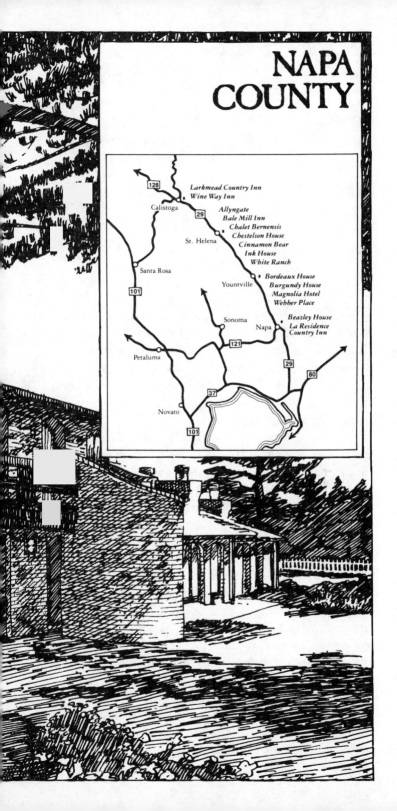

NAPA COUNTY

Larkmead Country Inn
Wine Way Inn

Calistoga

128

29

Allyngate
Bale Mill Inn
Chalet Bernensis
Chestelson House
Cinnamon Bear
Ink House
White Ranch

St. Helena

Santa Rosa

Bordeaux House
Burgundy House
Magnolia Hotel
Webber Place

Yountville

101

Sonoma

Napa

Beazley House
La Residence
Country Inn

121

Petaluma

29

80

37

Novato

101

Beazley House

1910 First Street
Napa, California 94558; (707) 257-1649

INNKEEPERS:	*Jim and Carol Beazley.*
ACCOMMODATIONS:	*Six rooms, one with private half bath; queen-size beds.*
RESERVATIONS:	*Four weeks recommended.*
MINIMUM STAY:	*Two nights on weekends.*
DEPOSIT:	*First night's lodging.*
CREDIT CARDS:	*MC, VISA.*
RATES:	*Moderate.*
RESTRICTIONS:	*No children. No pets.*

Fond memories of the Beazley House: friendly people (Jim and Carol Beazley), the smell of freshly baked muffins wafting from the kitchen, a warm and snuggly down comforter, and one of the finest old homes in Napa (an early California town with more than its share of distinguished literary and business personalities).

This two-story, Colonial Revival/Shingle-style house was built in 1902. Its hardwood floors, wainscoting, cove ceilings, and stained-glass windows bespeak its Edwardian origins. There's a large living room with a fireplace and a window flanked by bookshelves. (The Beazleys also keep plenty of games on hand: backgammon, chess, Yatzee, and dominoes are all available.) To the right of the music room is the formal dining room, where a breakfast of fresh fruits, home-baked muffins or bread and jams, coffee and tea, and fruit juice is served beginning promptly at 8:30 each morning. Guest rooms are individually decorated and named according to theme. In addition to the six accommodations currently offered, the carriage house will soon provide rooms with fireplaces and private baths.

The Beazleys are as comfortable and accommodating as their house. Both are unabashedly people-oriented. Carol served as a full-time nurse for fourteen years; Jim was a photo-journalist with the *Reno Evening*

Gazette and *Nevada State Journal*. A tour of b&b's in England and California left them with a confirmed belief in the owner-occupant philosophy of innkeeping. Many a stranger leaves Beazley House a friend — perhaps because this inn is a home as well as a business for its owners.

Beazley House is three blocks from central Napa, a city that is experiencing a rebirth as a tourist destination. It offers historic-architectural walking tours within the immediate area. There is also hot-air ballooning, cycling, gliding, horseback riding, and the Robert L. Stevenson Museum, all within a few miles. With its bright blue and white awnings, balanced symmetry and gracefully hipped roof, visitors will have no difficulty finding this attractive wine country inn. (It will soon be listed in the National Register of Historic Places.) But despite its impressive exterior, the best memories most people take away are of the warm and familylike atmosphere within. "We treat each individual not just as a customer," say the Beazleys, "but as a guest."

La Residence Country Inn

4066 St. Helena Highway North
Napa, California 94558; (707) 253-0337

INNKEEPER:	*Barbara Littenberg.*
ACCOMMODATIONS:	*Seven rooms, two with private bath; queen-size beds.*
RESERVATIONS:	*Two weeks recommended.*
MINIMUM STAY:	*None.*
DEPOSIT:	*First and last night's lodging.*
CREDIT CARDS:	*MC, VISA.*
RATES:	*Moderate to expensive.*
RESTRICTIONS:	*No children. No pets.*

L arry C. Parker was a river pilot in New Orleans in the 1840s who caught gold fever and arrived in San Francisco in 1849. A merchant in Stockton and San Francisco, he moved to Napa County in 1865 and took up farming. In 1870 he built his dream house, a Gothic Revival with a distinctly Southern flavor. Today his home still projects this amalgamation of regional styles, and the clientele attracted by its modern-day owners reflects the adventurous spirit of its original creator and inhabitant.

There is elegance here, as befits a home built by a man from the land of magnolias. Proprietor Barbara Littenberg has gone out of her way to furnish the rooms with antiques of the nineteenth century. (Her background as both fashion designer and archaeologist clearly is in evidence here.) The main library is well stocked with mysteries, with a preponderance of the English drawing room genre. (One room boasts a small library containing the works of Robert Louis Stevenson, the nineteenth-century English literary light who lived nearby.) Indeed, Barbara professes a strong preference for the English style of innkeeping, citing the White Moss Inn in the Lake District as the hostelry that has most influenced her own operation.

Bicycle enthusiasts will find a bike trail beginning right across the road. (It runs all the way to Yountville.)

Runners are encouraged to enjoy the fresh Napa air and sunshine on the same trail. Balloonists frequently stay here because of the proximity of the ballooning facilities, and the Littenbergs are happy to recommend tours at the local wineries. But if it's simply rest and relaxation you thirst after, you will not be disappointed. Each bedroom has its own sitting area, and the parklike setting gives the entire area a secluded and restful ambience. Its two acres boast magnolias (naturally), California live oaks, and orange, walnut, fig, apple, and pear trees.

The Continental breakfast of orange juice (fresh), coffee, croissants, and fresh fruit is served from 8:30 to 10:00 in the Breakfast Room. But you may find evenings at La Residence just as enjoyable; the Littenbergs are especially interested in serving an international clientele. "That's the part I like best," says Barbara. "Sitting around the parlor in the evening, sharing stories from all over the world." I'm sure the footloose Harry C. would approve.

Webber Place

6610 Webber Street
Yountville, California 94599; (707) 944-8384

INNKEEPER:	*Loren Holte.*
ACCOMMODATIONS:	*Four rooms, two with private bath; one cottage with private bath; double beds.*
RESERVATIONS:	*Three weeks recommended.*
MINIMUM STAY:	*None.*
DEPOSIT:	*First night's lodging.*
CREDIT CARDS:	*MC, VISA.*
RATES:	*Moderate.*
RESTRICTIONS:	*Children and/or pets in cottage only.*

Webber Place is a 1½-story Greek Revival, and a farmhouse. But what a farmhouse! This is the storybook clapboard farmhouse *par excellence,* complete with delicate white picket fence. Built by Sylvester and Polly Grigsby (descendants of Captain John Grigsby of the Bear Flag Revolt) in the 1850s, it was moved to its present station by one of the industrious Webber clan. Proprietor Loren Holte began work on it in the early 1970s. He has reconstructed almost the entire interior of this historic rust-red dwelling, while preserving many of the original accoutrements. (These include newspaper clippings from around the turn of the century, which Loren has framed and put on the walls; they were discovered during renovation.)

"It was just a piece of junk that nobody wanted," Loren says, recalling that he first heard of the Webber house through friends. This attractive bachelor is handy with a hammer, has a knack for decorating and a liking for antiques as well as people. At one point he took a six-month leave of absence from his job as a teacher at Napa State Hospital to work on his new acquisition. His work has paid off. Visitors are attracted by his friendliness as well as his taste in interiors, which run to American primitive and what Loren calls "American country."

One of several small miracles of reconstruction: over the years the wood paneling on the ceiling had been painted over several times. Loren simply flipped over each panel and carefully reattached it to the wood surface. The result was the intricate tongue and groove redwood paneling that graces many of the ceilings (and one wall) of the rooms.

The town of Yountville, in which Webber Place is located, is itself a small miracle of reconstruction. It was nothing more than a sleepy village containing a Veterans Hospital until a few years ago. Then Vintage 1870 — an attractive oasis of shops and boutiques — was opened by enterprising locals with an eye to attracting more of the tourist dollar. Employment went up, and the area received a face lift that in turn attracted other business catering to tourism. It now boasts four inns, several fine restaurants, and the Court of Two Sisters bakery.

Webber Place-isms I particularly liked: guests are greeted with wine from local wineries, such as Mondavi or Round Hill. There are fresh flowers in the rooms, and most rooms have old-fashioned, claw-foot bathtubs (some built for two, yet) on raised platforms, and pull-chain water closets. The lower suite is perfect for honeymooners, opening onto its private veranda with a private entrance as well. Wine and perishables may be stored in the refrigerator by guests; the Continental breakfast often includes homemade breads (the zucchini and the banana are both yummy).

There are plans for a gazebo in the backyard, and four new rooms will be added in the barn. Webber Place will be an interesting inn to keep an eye on.

Magnolia Hotel

6529 Yount Street
Yountville, California 94599; (707) 944-2056

INNKEEPERS:	Bruce and Bonnie Locken.
ACCOMMODATIONS:	Eleven rooms, all with private bath; twin, double, queen-, and king-size beds.
RESERVATIONS:	Two to three months for weekends.
MINIMUM STAY:	None.
DEPOSIT:	First and last night's lodging.
CREDIT CARDS:	Not accepted.
RATES:	Moderate to expensive.
RESTRICTIONS:	No children under sixteen. No pets.

I t was built as a hotel in 1873, of brick and native fieldstone — reputedly from the Silverado Trail. In the intervening years it has been a bordello, a hotel for laborers, a 4-H headquarters, and a speakeasy during Prohibition. It was rescued from oblivion by Ray and Nancy Monte (two of the creators of Vintage 1870) and is now owned by Bonnie and Bruce Locken, who have turned the Magnolia Hotel into one of the classiest and most fashionable country inns in the vineyards of California.

Class tells right from the moment one enters and spies the antique rolltop desk in the lobby. There is a parlor with a baby grand to gather about, if guests are in the mood for song as well as wine; the second floor has a very large deck, perfect for sipping wine and looking out over the surrounding vineyards. (The wine cellar is stocked with over three hundred California wines.) And there is an adjoining restaurant that numbers the redoubtable Julia Child as one of its champions. (*Travel/ Holiday* magazine has honored it for three years running.)

Each room has its own handmade theme doll created by Bonnie especially for that room. In the Magnolia Room I discovered a private balcony overlooking the heated pool. (I also found a welcome decanter of port wine.) There is a heated Jacuzzi with a redwood deck in the rear. My bedspread pattern was cleverly keyed to correspond to wall decor, and I liked the fireplace, the needlepoint chair design, and the pink lace curtains. (Other rooms have iron and brass beds, handmade quilts, and lace coverlets.) All rooms have a private tiled bath and plush towels, and it is worth noting that the Magnolia is air-conditioned during the summer.

Bruce Locken has long been in the hostelry trade, serving for thirty years at famous spots such as San Francisco's Clift Hotel. But he yearned for something different. "I wanted to get back to the small, intimate kind of operation — which is really how the business began," he says. He searched for eight years. In 1977 he found the Magnolia already in operation. It was love at first sight.

Bonnie is in charge of the kitchen, as one would expect from a professional who worked as a dietician for a chain of western hospitals. The restaurant is currently open Friday and Saturday only; there are two five-course entrées available, and four desserts.

For breakfast enjoy French toast baked in rounds; hot port wine syrup (they make it); sausage or double-thick bacon, from California Meat Company, one of the oldest sausage makers in San Francisco; fresh orange juice and eggs, baked or as an omelette (try New York sharp Cheddar cheese with mushrooms and sherry wine); and old-fashioned oatmeal with brown sugar, banana chips, and cream. (The breakfast is served in the restaurant on two family tables.)

If you can break away from the Lockens' famous collection of cookbooks, nearby attractions include a petrified forest, over a hundred wineries, a geyser named Old Faithful after its prototype in Yellowstone, and a mud bath (yes, a mud bath). The Lockens are happy to assist with reservations. This is an operation that marries the old with the very modern and makes it work.

Burgundy House

6711 Washington Street
Yountville, California 94599; (707) 944-2855

INNKEEPERS:	*Bob and Mary Keenan.*
ACCOMMODATIONS:	*Six rooms and two cottages, five with shared bath. Twin and double beds.*
RESERVATIONS:	*Six to eight weeks for summer and weekends.*
MINIMUM STAY:	*None.*
DEPOSIT:	*First night's lodging.*
CREDIT CARDS:	*AE, MC, VISA.*
RATES:	*Moderate.*
RESTRICTIONS:	*Children in cottages only. No pets.*

hen Charles Rouvegneau constructed this amazingly sturdy house from local fieldstone (walls are twenty-two inches thick, posts and beams handcut) in the early 1870s, he used it as the center of his winery and brandy-distilling operations. And he built it just as if he were in the Saône of his native France. One of Charles's happiest inspirations was a huge hearth in which he made bread daily to go with his best wine and brandy. Today you can eat breakfast in this same hearth area, and there's no more snug or cozy nook in all the Napa Valley.

Each room is uniquely appointed with antiques, many from the countryside of France. But they're not necessarily just for looking at. Feel free to buy that lamp you like so much; everything is for sale! In fact, that's how Bob and Mary Keenan got into the innkeeping business. Friends shopping at their antique store were forever in need of a place to stay, and the store gradually evolved into an inn.

Surrounding the inn are roses and an herb garden for the kitchen. During the summer months the shaded patio in the back proves a favorite spot for those who come to dawdle. The village of Yountville hasn't grown much in population in the last hundred years, but it is a pleasant place in which to stroll any time of year. There was a bit too much chill in the air the night I visited, however, so I settled for enjoying a crackling fire in the long, narrow common room downstairs.

No doubt about it: there's a French ambience here — nineteenth-century French at that. Burgundy House's sign contains a vignette of Napoleon III, a reminder of its French — or at least French-American — origins. It is one of the few older inns built exclusively of stone on this coast.

Later I relaxed in my room, pampered by silk sheets and a lush patterned comforter on my brass bed, enjoying the flower paintings on the wall and the decanted wine on the bureau. The moon was struggling to stay out, and in its cloudy light I could see Cabernet, Reisling, and Chardonnay vineyards from my window, as grey as the Grey Reisling I was drinking. Wine country, indeed!

Breakfast came early around a pine table in the hearth room below. Danish pastry, a fresh fruit platter (which sometimes includes strawberries in hollowed-out pineapples and stewed rhubarb in clear glass dishes), coffee, and my favorite, tangy fresh-squeezed OJ. It wasn't until I was ready to leave that I discovered two of the Keenans' most delightful secrets. One was their collection of antique games. The other was a remarkably *naïve* antique French birdcage.

There was another touch I particularly liked. No clocks. "Guests shouldn't have to worry about time," Mary avows firmly. *J'en veux plus!* Would that other inns would copy this. A most unusual and discerning place.

Bordeaux House

6600 Washington Street
Yountville, California 94599; (707) 944-2855

INNKEEPERS:	*Bob and Mary Keenan.*
ACCOMMODATIONS:	*Six rooms, all with private bath; twin and queen-size beds.*
RESERVATIONS:	*Two months for Saturday night.*
MINIMUM STAY:	*None.*
DEPOSIT:	*First night's lodging.*
CREDIT CARDS:	*AE, MC, VISA.*
RATES:	*Moderate to expensive.*
RESTRICTIONS:	*No pets.*

If Burgundy House is the Keenans' *beau ideal* of the traditional French country inn transplanted to California, Bordeaux House is their *beau geste,* their no-holds-barred experiment with the ultra-modern. What a wildly contrasting pair of inns — both owned by the same couple! Bordeaux House is not only contemporary; its fine, clean brick lines are downright futuristic. Where Burgundy House lulls us with artfully recreated memories of things past, Bordeaux openly titil-lates us with visions of a California future. *Star Wars* creator George Lucas could do worse than to hire this couple if he ever needs an intergalactic b&b for his space fables.

Evocation of the future was exactly what architect Bob Keenan had in mind when he designed Bordeaux House. "I wanted something that would be a classic a hundred years from now, just like Burgundy House is today." All beds are on raised platforms (good for people with back trouble, incidentally); mirrors are ringed with soft makeup lights. The furniture is Italian contemporary.

The colors tend toward camel and burgundy. In my room the table was Plexiglas, as were the bathroom fixtures. Tailored fabrics are much in evidence; the lamps are mostly brass. Near my fireplace was a potted palm, a little triumph of audacity much in keeping with the rest of the tongue-in-cheek, yet decidedly relaxing decor.

Which is one of the effects the Keenans aimed to achieve. "We wanted rooms where a person can go and not be distracted by anything," Bob says. The aura of highly personalized simplicity present here is relaxing in ways the untrained eye may not always consciously perceive.

Daughter Jean is responsible for the wall graphics in the main living area. (Much of the original art here is her work.) The rooms have fresh flowers, a fireplace, a balcony, a private bath and patio, and a carafe of wine; the Keenans also put out lemon juice for those who are "thirsty after tasting wine all day."

Although coffee is served in the living area, guests go to Burgundy House for breakfast. The effect is magical. One slips out of the future and races straight back into the past without ever having passed Go. The two old Italian stone pines out in front add to the feeling of pleasant unreality.

A certain lightheartedness seems to cling to this inn, and is reflected in the kind of people who stay here. Mary recalls a party of ten who hid in a closet to surprise a birthday guest. Before you could say "Don Giovanni," the pranksters had gotten themselves locked in. And there they stayed—until the birthday friend arrived to let them out, much later than expected.

Throughout my stay here I kept searching for the one word that would best describe Bordeaux House. That word is *sophistication*. Thank you, Bob and Mary Keenan! If the future is anything like your fine inn, we haven't too much to worry about.

The Ink House

1575 St. Helena Highway
St. Helena, California 94574; (707) 963-3890

INNKEEPER:	*Lois Clark.*
ACCOMMODATIONS:	*Three rooms, all with shared bath; double beds.*
RESERVATIONS:	*Two weeks recommended.*
MINIMUM STAY:	*Two nights on weekends.*
DEPOSIT:	*Full amount.*
CREDIT CARDS:	*Not accepted.*
RATES:	*Moderate.*
RESTRICTIONS:	*No children under 12. No pets.*

T heron H. Ink, who built this huge and decidedly Italianate Victorian, operated not one but several vineyards, as well as ranches and a livery stable. He was a landholder in Marin, Sonoma, and Napa counties, serving as a Napa County supervisor for many years.

Ink House is still very much a private residence. (Guests use the parlor and dining room and lounge on the wide, wrap-around porch.) Proprietor Lois Clark and her husband George raised five children here, and it was when the children had left the nest that the bed and breakfast idea took hold. It's not hard to see why: Theron H. built this square, brown, white-trimmed residence on a palatial scale. Double stairways made it possible to divide the house in halves, one of which is for guests and the other for the Clarks.

There is no sign outside. (Lois doesn't want people who come just to gawk.) Once inside it took me some time to get used to the scale. (Ceilings are twelve feet high.) In the parlor I discovered a huge antique pump organ. The bathroom — shared by all guests — was the size of a Roman bath; I was told it was once a bedroom.

My room was pink, with a brass-trimmed iron bed, white lace curtains, pink towels, and flowered wallpaper. The only truly modern touch here was the electric blanket — one that I genuinely appreciated.

Clever Lois keeps a book in which visitors are encouraged to review local restaurants, the better to inform you of which eateries are currently in favor. Lois's own Continental breakfast (served at 8:30) consists of juice, coffee, nut bread, and fruit. The bread is baked by Lois — she got in the habit of baking her own bread while she was raising her children.

Lois's most amusing moment as an innkeeper came the morning after Halloween when three young couples left a stuffed, three-armed monster at the breakfast table for her to find. She is a believer in intuition where guests are concerned. "You get a feeling for people — some want to talk, and some want to be left alone."

The Ink House is a place apart, a fascinating and very pleasant curiosity. What makes it interesting is its bold combination of styles. Its monumental scale seems to promise a kind of anonymity, yet what it ultimately delivers is a warm intimacy. The Ink House is finally a home, not a palace — but then Lois Clark could have told you that.

The White Ranch

707 White Lane
St. Helena, California 94574; (707) 963-4635

INNKEEPER:	Ruth Davis.
ACCOMMODATIONS:	One room with private bath.
RESERVATIONS:	Two months recommended.
MINIMUM STAY:	None.
DEPOSIT:	$25 to $50.
CREDIT CARDS:	Not accepted.
RATES:	Moderate.
RESTRICTIONS:	No children. No pets.

T alk about individual attention! You'll get it here for sure, because this delightful bed and breakfast caters to just one person (or couple) at a time. There is a private entrance to the bedroom; and although there may be only one (or two) of you, proprietor Ruth Davis maintains a dressing room and a private bath for the comfort of her visitors.

This lovely farm dwelling was built in 1865 by Asa White, a pioneer Methodist minister. (He arrived with his family in a covered wagon.) This is deep country: you are far enough from the highway not to hear traffic sounds. You *might* hear the sound of roosters cheerfully crowing you awake of a morning, and there are plenty of other farm animals to keep you company. (There are horses pastured here, and turkeys are kept in the barn.) Ancient walnut trees in the front yard complete the bucolic scene.

Ruth's accommodations are really closer to a certain kind of European-style bed and breakfast experience than many of the others toured. (In Europe and the British Isles a bed and breakfast establishment is just as likely to be somebody's home with a spare room as an inn.) One of the objectives of this arrangement is to cut down on the expense of hotels; but it also allows the guests to find out how the people of an area or region live and think. There's no better way to get close to people than to live in their home.

Ruth embarked on her bed and breakfasting adventure when her friend Lois Clark at the Ink House called to say she had a honeymoon couple — and no room at the inn, as it were. Ruth obliged by taking them in, and she's been at it ever since.

Anyone who's ever spent time on a farm will love her porch swing. There's a picnic table on the lawn; the parlor has a fireplace and a fine Queen Anne table and chairs. The guest room is furnished with heirlooms of Ruth's family. (Her grandmother's crocheted quilt is on the bed.) I liked the oversize mirror on the dressing table, too.

There is a small porch off the bedroom with a wooden bench for those who wish to sit and drink in the country silence. But I went to bed early, and my sleep was bone-deep and satisfying. I woke up, refreshed and ravenous, to the sound of roosters; Ruth presented me with homemade nut bread, popovers, orange juice, fresh fruit, and espresso. Delicious!

Traffic, job, crime, and noise pollution got you down? I recommend the White Ranch as the perfect antidote for your city blues.

Chalet Bernensis

225 St. Helena Highway
St. Helena, California 94574; (707) 963-4423

INNKEEPERS:	*Jack and Essie Doty.*
ACCOMMODATIONS:	*Nine rooms, four with private bath; twin, double, and queen-size beds.*
RESERVATIONS:	*Three months recommended.*
MINIMUM STAY:	*Two nights on weekends.*
DEPOSIT:	*First night's lodging.*
CREDIT CARDS:	*MC, VISA.*
RATES:	*Moderate.*
RESTRICTIONS:	*No children under fifteen. No pets.*

S t. Helena is indisputably one of the prettiest towns in the Napa Valley. And Chalet Bernensis is one of the nicest inns you'll find here, or anywhere else. Built in 1884 by John Thomann — he operated the Sutter Home Winery next door — it has been lovingly restored by Jack and Essie Doty. The original water tower (a common sight in the California countryside) has been carefully replicated and four of the inn's nine rooms are here.

The Sutter Home Winery is still in operation. Just a few steps away, it seems a perfect place to begin one's wine-tasting activities. (Or festivities, as the case may be.) Other wineries within walking distance are Louis Martini, Sattui, and Heitz. Prestigious Inglenook and Christian Brothers are only a few miles away.

Chalet Bernensis is still very much a mansion — or rather an estate, as nineteenth-century vintners were fond of calling their winemaking fiefdoms. The grounds are spacious, with a long curved driveway. Gables are much in evidence. It is easy to imagine high-prancing horses and many-fringed surreys arriving with wealthy guests, as servants pour glasses of estate-bottled bubbly. Today guests arrive in a different kind of carriage, but the Victorian opulence lingers on.

All the rooms have antiques. Some bathrooms have claw-foot tubs and pedestal sinks, and many have fireplaces. I found my bed one of the most comfortable I had slept in on my tour. (My somnolence was enhanced by the presence of a lovely handmade quilt.) Breakfast was served between 8:30 and 10:00 A.M.: homemade scones (or muffins), fresh fruit, juices, and homemade jams and jellies, coffee and tea.

Although the Dotys have menus of all nearby restaurants on hand, you may wish to picnic on one of the picnic tables on the grounds. Or you might wish to take in the Silverado museum, or enjoy the Calistoga hot springs. Touring has always been a part of this house; old photos from the 1880s demonstrate clearly that trolleys and trains came almost up to John Thomann's front door, loaded with the affluent and not-so-affluent on their way to Calistoga and its reputedly miraculous mineral waters.

Early wine merchants like John Thomann were classic bourgeois in the best sense. Like the medieval Florentines and the seventeenth-century Dutch, their nineteenth-century world was unapologetically elegant, yet essentially practical; homes were beautiful, but also the center of businesses, and of family life. Chalet Bernensis is a window onto that refined yet industrious sensibility that influenced California so much then — and still does.

Chestelson House

1417 Kearney Street
St. Helena, California 94574; (707) 963-2238

INNKEEPER:	*Claudia Chestelson.*
ACCOMMODATIONS:	*Two rooms, both with private bath; queen and king-size beds.*
RESERVATIONS:	*Three to four weeks.*
MINIMUM STAY:	*Three nights.*
DEPOSIT:	*Full amount.*
CREDIT CARDS:	*Not accepted.*
RATES:	*Moderate.*
RESTRICTIONS:	*No children. No pets.*

This understated but instantly intriguing Victorian may not have a past, or then again it may. Proprietor Claudia Chestelson awaits the definitive historian to sort out the welter of conflicting legends and hearsay that surround her home. But Chestelson House really doesn't need a past to capture the imagination. It has the vivacious, endlessly energetic Ms. Chestelson — and she's enough to relax and entertain even the most hard-pressed of workaholics.

She has given much thought to her bed and breakfast philosophy. "When you take people into your home, you are really doing something rather intimate — you are dealing with the most intimate aspects of people's lives." She pauses, and continues: "What you offer them — along with the intimacy — is a kind of elegance." She shrugs and laughs. "Nursemaid, psychologist, decorator — just say I offer free decorating tips and advice to the lovelorn."

Along with her unfailing taste and *joie de vivre*, Claudia also offers sherry in the rooms and is always happy to help with winery and restaurant reservations. My room was the front guest room. Definitely part of a home — but what attention to detail! A French armoire, a bay window with white shutters, a queen-size bed with a white comforter, a brass bedstead, an oval mirror

with a wood frame — and fresh flowers, of course. (The bath is private but separate.)

Breakfast was pineapple with strawberries, pastries from the Court of Two Sisters bakery, French coffee with a touch of cinnamon, or tea. It arrived at the good, leisurely hour of 9:00 A.M. in the country kitchen (breakfast is also available in the main sitting room).

But watch out if you are single. Claudia loves bringing people together. One Marin County couple fell in love here and decided to get married; they spent their wedding night at Chestelson House. (And came back to celebrate their first anniversary.)

There is a fine view of St. Helena's surrounding hills. And St. Helena remains a permanent fascination for those who like to explore the picturesque and out of the way. The restaurants (Miramonte, Domaine Chandon, French Laundry) are expensive but justly famous. And if you just like to sit with coffee or sherry on the wraparound veranda, you'll find that as pleasant as any of the local attractions.

Claudia Chestelson likes to give her guests personal attention, and it is her prodigious talent for pampering that makes the hours spent in her home such a memorable — and joyful — experience.

The Cinnamon Bear

1407 Kearney Street
St. Helena, California 94574; (707) 963-4653

INNKEEPER:	*Genny Jenkins.*
ACCOMMODATIONS:	*Four rooms, all with private bath; double beds.*
RESERVATIONS:	*2 to 4 weeks.*
MINIMUM STAY:	*None.*
DEPOSIT:	*Full amount.*
CREDIT CARDS:	*Not accepted.*
RATES:	*Moderate.*
RESTRICTIONS:	*No children. No pets.*

T his lovely family home was built in 1904 as a wedding present to Susan Metzner from her father. Husband Walter Metzner was mayor of St. Helena for twenty years, and he lived with Susan in their comfortable home at 1407 Kearney Street until 1970. The present owner and creator of the Cinnamon Bear, Genny Jenkins, purchased the house in 1971 to provide a home for three growing children.

This resourceful woman initiated (and still maintains) her own insurance business. The bed and breakfast idea developed when oldest son David went to England and came back with enthusiastic reports of bed and breakfasts abroad. "So when the kids went to college," Genny says jokingly, "I changed the locks and rented out their rooms."

There was more to it than that, of course. It took tasteful, systematic remodeling of each room to provide the necessary facilities while giving each room its own character. The house had much character to begin with: broad wraparound porches — used for breakfast and general socializing in earlier days, as today — handcrafted redwood paneling, and a sitting room as well as a dining room all testify to the quality of life of its previous owners.

Mirrored built-ins, redwood beam ceilings, and ample bay windows covered by delicate lace curtains add to the homey elegance. The day I visited, there was a cheerful fire in the fireplace, plenty of games, sherry, and good books — and a most important staple of the bed and breakfast trade (and one that many forget): rocking chairs.

My room was similarly redolent of both taste and comfort: Persian rugs in tones of blue and burgundy. A white and burgundy comforter and pillow shams. A beige and brown private bath with a special country feeling. And, of course, bears: they are present in all sizes and variations throughout the house, although Genny is careful not to overdo the motif.

Breakfast is hearty — very much so. Homemade breads, fresh fruit, coffee freshly ground in an antique coffee mill, OJ, and — a real English country feast of eggs, meat, and potatoes! Breakfast is served in either the large dining room or on the porch (if weather permits). A nice touch of Americana: if the aroma of delicious food and fresh-brewed coffee doesn't waken you, the school bell next door will.

Genny likes to tell of the time she booked a couple over the phone and was then unexpectedly detained downtown. "The husband literally took over. When I got home a fire was lit, additional reservations had been made, wine poured, cheese served, and messages taken. Not only that — when I finally got back, he assumed I was a guest and proceeded to show me to my room." And where did the couple sleep? "In the basement — he'd booked all the available rooms!"

Friendly and *welcome* are two words that describe the Cinnamon Bear, a bed and breakfast that owes much of its appeal to the house — but most of it to the warm and enterprising woman who makes it a home.

Allyngate

1321 Allyn Avenue
St. Helena, California 94574; (707) 963-2848

INNKEEPER:	*Sharon Black.*
ACCOMMODATIONS:	*Three rooms, one with private bath; queen-size beds.*
RESERVATIONS:	*Two weeks recommended.*
MINIMUM STAY:	*None.*
DEPOSIT:	*Full amount.*
CREDIT CARDS:	*Not accepted.*
RATES:	*Moderate.*
RESTRICTIONS:	*No children. No pets.*

Here's a quiet, understated place perfect for three couples who want a weekend in the country together. The house is one hundred years old and was built as a two-family dwelling. (One half is now used by proprietor Sharon Black; the other consists of the three rooms for guests.)

The architecture is Carpenter Gothic; the neighborhood is very quiet. Furnishings are a nice mix of English and American antiques. Sharon Black, the proprietor, is an elementary school teacher who genuinely enjoys meeting people. She found her dream house by "wandering around until I found a house big enough for friends as well as family."

One guest room has a corner fireplace, as does the parlor. Wine is served in the afternoon, and there is a pantry for guests to use. (Ice buckets, wineglasses, plastic forks, bottle openers, and picnic baskets and dishes are all available.) Sharon is currently constructing a sun porch on which to serve her breakfasts of homemade muffins or coffee cake, fruits in season, fresh-squeezed orange juice, and coffee.

Breakfast is a touchy subject with many bed and breakfast owners and operators these days. The villains of the piece are certain over-zealous county health inspectors who have gone so far as to insist that proprietors must have commercial kitchens to bake homemade bread and muffins! Angry owners have so far won this round — referred to locally as "the battle of the muffins."

Sharon is on the board of directors of the new Napa Valley Bed and Breakfast Association, headed by James Beazley of Beazley House, in the city of Napa. The association will strive to set proper standards for local bed and breakfast operations — and possibly function as a loyal opposition to zealots in certain government agencies.

My favorite room was downstairs, with a corner fireplace. There were white lace curtains and a cluster of old framed photos of Sharon's Grandfather Allyn. An old "handcrank" Singer sewing machine sits on the table. Salmon, rose, blue, brown, and beige tones are included in the color scheme (there are matching comforter and pillow shams); the wallpaper is a delicate rose pattern on a beige and white background. Understated — and very nice.

It's not every day that one has the opportunity to stay at a fine bed and breakfast inn and strike a blow for freedom at the same time. (Commercial kitchens for homemade bread and muffins, indeed!) Come and encourage Sharon and her colleagues in their struggle against the regulatory vigilantes. Long may they bake!

Bale Mill Inn

3431 North St. Helena Highway
St. Helena, California 94574; (707) 963-4545

INNKEEPER:	*Tom Scheibal.*
ACCOMMODATIONS:	*Five rooms, three with private bath; double beds.*
RESERVATIONS:	*Three weeks.*
MINIMUM STAY:	*None.*
DEPOSIT:	*Full amount.*
CREDIT CARDS:	*MC, VISA.*
RATES:	*Inexpensive to moderate.*
RESTRICTIONS:	*No children under six. No pets.*

T he Bale Mill is a literary inn — and a place with a considerable sense of humor. Rooms are named and decorated after American literary figures. But don't let the reasonable prices and my descriptions of the whimsey and easy elegance here fool you; this is a very classy operation. Although proprietor Tom Scheibal has been in business only a short time, his establishment has already been chosen as the top country inn in the Napa Valley by Macy's, which featured it extensively in an advertising campaign built around a wine country inn theme.

Emily Dickinson's room is decorated like the porch of a New England country home — bravo, Tom! (Her room also contains original wicker pieces and a love seat — a poignant choice, considering her lifelong self-isolation from the bustling New England world outside her shuttered windows.) Jack London (whose home was only a few miles away in Glen Ellen) is recalled by souvenirs of various heroic adventures, Indian relics, hilariously campy furniture — and a wolf under the bed.

Teddy Roosevelt is honored by crossed flags and antiques from his period. (There is a bugle on which a guest once played a muffled "charge" in the middle of the night.) The Captain Quinn room is the cabin of an imaginary character of nineteenth-century adventure-before-the-mast fiction of Robert Louis Stevenson and Melville.

(And created, one suspects, for the delight of Tom's young son, Quinn.) All rooms have a private deck and patio.

My favorite is the Hemingway room. It replicates a hotel room in Papa's beloved Key West (the ceiling fan revolves at a snail's pace; the floor is limed), but it is also a repository of effects and memorabilia that reflect the writer's career — and preoccupations (war canteen, safari helmet, mounted bull's horns). A hula dancer lamp, a potted palm, and shutters on the windows further suggest his Caribbean haunts and adventures.

Tom considers the Napa Valley healthier for his son than the city (the inn's environs include the historic bale mill after which the inn is named, a state park, moped rentals, golf, tennis, horseback riding and swimming). Breakfast at Bale Mill is certainly healthy: Tom's homemade cinnamon bread, pastries, fresh fruit, fresh-squeezed orange juice, and coffee. With rooms furnished with antiques from the time periods of famous American authors, what more could a tired and hungry writer like myself possibly want?

This is a reasonably priced and extremely original bed and breakfast experience that even nonwriters shouldn't miss. Go now, before the mobs arrive — as they surely will.

Larkmead Country Inn

1103 Larkmead Lane
Calistoga, California 94515; (707) 942-5360

INNKEEPERS:	*Gene and Joan Garbarino.*
ACCOMMODATIONS:	*Four rooms, all with shared bath; double and twin beds.*
RESERVATIONS:	*Four to five weeks for weekends.*
MINIMUM STAY:	*None.*
DEPOSIT:	*First night's lodging.*
CREDIT CARDS:	*VISA.*
RATES:	*Moderate.*
RESTRICTIONS:	*No children. No pets.*

Gene and Joan Garbarino don't have a sign out front, and they don't advertise their inn — they don't have to. Most of their bookings are repeat business and the rest come by word of mouth. People who like this place tend to like it very much; it's not hard to see why. Classical yet simple, in a tranquil setting literally in the heart of a vineyard, perhaps the best word to describe Larkmead Country Inn is *serene*.

This inn on old Larkmead Lane is located next to famed Hanns Kornell Champagne Cellars; it was built by the son of an earlier vintner, on the occasion of his marriage. The house abounds with antiques, paintings, and prints from the Garbarinos' collection; Persian carpets, broad porches, wide clapboards, and a certain atmosphere of unperturbable solidity all suggest a New England inn. Until one looks out the window, that is: all rooms overlook row on row of vineyards.

It is not particularly surprising, then, that all rooms are named after wines of the Napa Valley. The Beaujolais has an antique sewing machine and a private porch from which you see all the way to the hills on the edge of the valley on a clear and moonlit night. The Chardonnay Room features antique brass twin beds, white wicker chairs, red and white flowered spreads — and the fresh flowers and complimentary decanter of wine that all guests receive.

It so happens that my favorite room here is also my favorite wine. The elegant Chenin Blanc Room has a chaise lounge I loved, curtains and matching wallpaper, an armoire, a white wicker chair and table — and a very comfy double bed. The living room is comfortable, too — Joan's afternoon tea was especially pleasant in front of a blazing fire in the fireplace. The Garbarinos have chess, cards, puzzles, dominoes, and many books on hand to occupy the idle hand and mind.

Breakfast is served on one of the porches, when weather permits; mine arrived in the dining room. (And it arrived on fine china with sterling silver and linen napkins, I might add.) It consisted of fresh fruit, freshly ground coffee, and a basket of croissants, scones, and French rolls with sweet butter and homemade preserves.

The Garbarinos are from Orinda; Gene is a dentist. Both feel that their part of the Napa Valley is especially beautiful at harvest time. And both are happy to be serving the public in such a direct and personal way. "When's the last time you heard of a hotel receiving a thank-you note?" Joan asks. She adds with a touch of awe: "I've received twenty-three!"

That's as good a definition as any I've heard of the difference between a hotel and the bed and breakfast experience.

Wine Way Inn

1019 Foothill Boulevard, Highway 29
Calistoga, California 94515; (707) 942-0680

INNKEEPERS:	*Allen and Dede Good.*
ACCOMMODATIONS:	*Four rooms, two with private bath; double and queen-size beds.*
RESERVATIONS:	*Four weeks recommended for weekends in April and November.*
MINIMUM STAY:	*Two nights.*
DEPOSIT:	*Full amount.*
CREDIT CARDS:	*Not accepted.*
RATES:	*Moderate.*
RESTRICTIONS:	*Children discouraged. No pets.*

A llen and Dede Good had always wanted to work together in a joint venture, and Dede had stayed at bed and breakfasts in Europe. While vacationing in Napa Valley in 1980, they talked to a realtor. Only a few short months later, they had relocated from Los Angeles and opened their doors to the bed and breakfast public. Both continue their careers (she is a director of occupational therapy at a rehabilitation center; he manages an auto body shop) but both are vigorous proponents of the owner-operated school of innkeeping.

Their house, built in 1915 as a family home, has many of the characteristics of a country house: the Mayacamas Mountains come right down to meet the redwood deck in back. Rooms are named after towns on Highway 29, the main wine country route. St. Helena — the room where I slept, and my favorite — has a bed fit for a queen (and in fact is queen size), a private bath, an armoire, and — an especially nice touch — a basket of colored yarn compatible with the patchwork quilt on the bed. (Dede later told me it came from her home in Indiana.) There was also a candle and candlestick, a piece which more inns should consider placing in their rooms for those of us who find candlelight relaxing just before bedtime.

The comfortable living room sports a cozy fireplace, English china and pottery, an antique clock on the mantel, and (the day I was there) a decanter of excellent Inglenook Chablis. For those who enjoy excursions, Dede is happy to prepare a "hobo picnic": everything but wine for guests to take on their winery tours (including a picnic cloth for the table).

This poised and attractive couple get around to local restaurants, and are glad to share first-hand impressions, as well as to make reservations. "We conduct a service for travelers in the area," Dede says, "and if they want help finding their way around, we provide it." Both she and her husband are quick to add that if the guest's first priority is privacy, that preference is strictly observed.

Local attractions include the Sharpsteen Museum (memorabilia, antiques, and photographs of Calistoga from its glory days as a flourishing resort of the 1860s) and a petrified forest. Why not try a mud bath? It's inexpensive and relaxing, and an experience you won't soon forget. (Just don't let friends take pictures, or you may never hear the end of it.)

Breakfast at Wine Way is Continental: croissants, fruit of the season, fresh-squeezed orange juice, home-made cakes and pastries, and coffee. And get this, sleepy-heads: if you're too beat from the previous day's wine tasting, breakfast will be served to you in bed. Now, that's luxury.

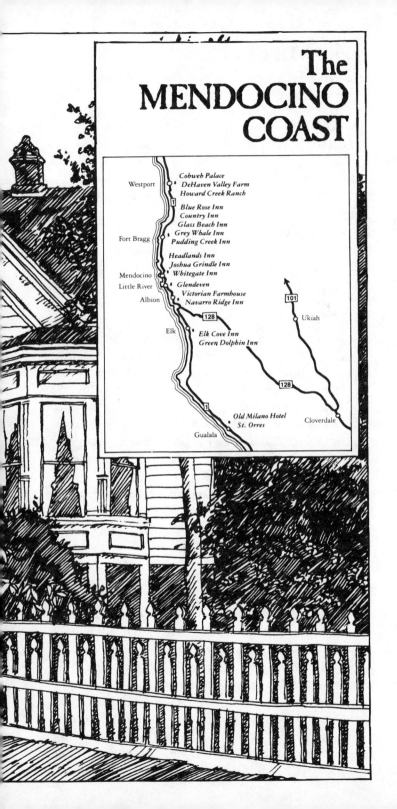

The
MENDOCINO
COAST

Westport
- Cobweb Palace
- DeHaven Valley Farm
- Howard Creek Ranch

Fort Bragg
- Blue Rose Inn
- Country Inn
- Glass Beach Inn
- Grey Whale Inn
- Pudding Creek Inn

Mendocino
- Headlands Inn
- Joshua Grindle Inn
- Whitegate Inn

Little River
- Glendeven
- Victorian Farmhouse

Albion
- Navarro Ridge Inn

Elk
- Elk Cove Inn
- Green Dolphin Inn

101
Ukiah

128

128

Gualala
- Old Milano Hotel
- St. Orres

Cloverdale

Old Milano Hotel

38300 Highway One
Gualala, California 95445; (707) 884-3256

INNKEEPERS:	*Theodora and Bruce McBroom.*
ACCOMMODATIONS:	*Ten rooms, four with private bath; double beds.*
RESERVATIONS:	*Four weeks recommended.*
MINIMUM STAY:	*Two nights on weekends.*
DEPOSIT:	*First night's lodging.*
CREDIT CARDS:	*MC, VISA.*
RATES:	*Moderate to expensive.*
RESTRICTIONS:	*No children. No pets.*

I n 1905 Bert Luccinetti built a restaurant and pub on a cliff overhanging Castle Rock, alongside what was then a busy railroad and stage road. (It catered mainly to lumbermen.) New owners made it into a resort for fishermen in the 1920s; the 1950s saw it modernized, its Victorian heritage obscured by various layers of ticky-tacky "improvements." It was discovered by Theodora and Bruce McBroom a few years ago and is now one of the most highly regarded inns on the northern California coast.

Bruce McBroom is a well-known Hollywood photographer, Mrs. McBroom one of filmdom's best costume designers. (Some of her credits include *Godfather II, Myra Breckinridge,* and *Bonnie and Clyde.*) Both put their considerable skills to work in this impressive blend of old and new. The Old Milano is now recorded in the National Register of Historic Places.

The rooms are named after Italian operas. There are two cottages — and a caboose where the old railroad once ran. It has walls of sandblasted wood, a galley, and a red pot-bellied stove. Two brakemen's seats for taking in the sunsets can be reached by a ladder.

Beds, bureaus, tables, lampshades, quilts, and bric-a-brac have been chosen with the care of a casting director. Morris wallpapers, original paintings, redwood wainscoting in the halls, and old-fashioned car-sided ceilings are also featured. The bed in which Merle Oberon "died" in the film version of *Wuthering Heights* is in the room called La Forza del Destino. You will also see Eastlake chairs, Tiffany lamps galore, and a sofa that was the first Riviera bed made in 1906.

The gracious Wine Parlor is made cheerful by a great stone fireplace. Adjacent are the quieter and more reflective comforts of the Music Room; *aficionados* of art books will find a fine collection. The staff of the Old Milano includes certified massage practitioners, according to its brochure. Another of the more comfortable concessions to modern sensibilities is a hot tub facing the ocean. (It is encircled by an old-fashioned knob-topped fence for privacy.)

The Cavalliera Rusticana room, with its breathtaking ocean view, was my favorite. The William Morris wallpaper design is in shades of blue, lilac, pink, and green. There's a comfortable over-stuffed rocker facing the tumultuous Pacific. An oval wood-framed mirror and fresh flowers in a pitcher complete the feeling of restful privacy.

Breakfast consists of unique homemade breads (Ukrainian poppy seed cake and banana coconut), sweet butter and cream cheese, and locally roasted coffee and tea. Guests may have their breakfast on the loggia, in the gardens, or in bed.

I left the Old Milano revitalized. Its setting is sensational, but the main ingredient of its success is the taste of its owners. There is something dreamlike in its unique compound of the Victorian and the modern. The Old Milano is like an image from film art made real, and its restfulness is to a large extent due to its ability to make us feel that we are a part of another, more ordered world.

St. Orres

36601 Highway One
Gualala, California 95445; (707) 884-3303

INNKEEPERS:	Ted Black, Rich Wasserman, Eric Black, Rosemary Campiformio.
ACCOMMODATIONS:	Eight rooms and three cottages, three rooms with private bath; double and queen-size beds.
RESERVATIONS:	Three months for weekends.
MINIMUM STAY:	Two nights in cottages on the weekends.
DEPOSIT:	Full amount.
CREDIT CARDS:	MC, VISA.
RATES:	Moderate to expensive.
RESTRICTIONS:	Children in cottages only. No pets.

The windswept isolation and wild charm of this part of the Mendocino coast is staggering. The environs (not to mention the elements) seem to demand one of two architectural styles: rigorous simplicity or the same spendthrift abandon that nature has lavished on her handiwork in the area. Master craftsperson Eric Black opted for the latter. The result is a fantasy, an explosion of fine art, and an architectural wonder.

It was just a few years ago that he and carpenter Richard Wasserman bought the remains of the old Seaside Hotel (built in the 1920s) and went to work on it. Oregon red cedar was used to transform the exterior, topped off by twin domed towers, deliberately reminiscent of the homeland of the Russian trappers who settled the area. Is it any wonder that passersby stop to marvel at this audacious Russophilic beauty in the wilderness?

The fairy-tale extravagance continues inside. The entrance hall has some very fine Art Nouveau and Edwardian pieces, and highly detailed stained-glass windows. The sitting room is dominated by a castle-size fireplace that looks like it belongs in Charles Laughton's

Henry the Eighth banquet scene. (And *six* oak doors, with stained-glass windows in each.) The dining room rises a dizzying three stories to an octagonal dome above, with row on row of windows culminating in a single rank of stained-glass panes just below its copper-domed crown.

The two front rooms have direct ocean views and French doors that open onto a balcony. Most rooms share baths "down the hall" — a His, a Hers, and a spacious Ours with tiled tub enclosures and dual shower heads. Quilts by St. Helena quilt maker Anne Kessler are lush velvet; rooms have intricate redwood paneling. (Even the telephone is paneled in redwood.)

The newest accommodation is the Tree House. This experiment in luxury contains a lovely queen-size brass bed, a tile bath with a deep sunken tub, a carpet, and its own kitchenette. As if that weren't enough, there is a Franklin stove fireplace with a hand-painted tile hearth; the living room has an ocean view, with French doors leading onto a sun deck.

Other than Rosemary Campiformio's long standing enjoyment in serving people, none of the four friends (Ted Black is Eric's uncle) had any inn or restaurant experience when they began. This has not handicapped them. Their restaurant and its chef Leif Benson already have achieved a considerable reputation. The complimentary breakfast for guests is from 8:30 to 9:30 and consists of homemade pastries, yogurt, nuts, raisins, and fresh fruit juices.

For me the words that best describe St. Orres are *magic* and *extravagance.* And perhaps the most wonderful part of it are the genuinely reasonable prices.

Elk Cove Inn

6300 South Highway One
Elk, California 95432; (707) 877-3321

INNKEEPERS:	Michael and Hildrun-Uta Boynoff.
ACCOMMODATIONS:	Eight rooms, six with private bath; double and queen-size beds.
RESERVATIONS:	Two weeks recommended for weekends.
MINIMUM STAY:	None.
DEPOSIT:	$50 to $100.
CREDIT CARDS:	Not accepted.
RATES:	Expensive.
RESTRICTIONS:	No children under eight. No pets.

This sweet Victorian was built in the early 1890s by the L.E. White Lumber Company. (L.E. built it for his son, who was the superintendent of his mill.) From 1890 to the crash in 1929 the nearby hamlet of Elk was a booming lumber port. Now it is the quintessential sleepy coast village. And this small but charming bed and breakfast inn is the archetypical Mendocino bed and breakfast — provided you come here to get away from everything. Because there is nothing — literally *nothing* — to do here but walk, read, eat, and sleep. If it is a period of total rest you are looking for, this is definitely the place for you.

Hildrun was born in Germany but was brought to this country early in life; she is a skilled cook, specializing in European cookery (dinner is served here as well as breakfast). She met Michael — to whom she has been married for three years — and invited him to a picnic on July 4, 1977. "He came late — and never left," Hildrun says. The Boynoffs are friendly, cosmopolitan, and very amusing people whose talent for entertaining is a central attraction of their operation.

"What we strive for is giving people things they don't do for themselves at home," Hildrun says, "yet in a

way that makes them *feel* like they are at home." Which is, by the way, perhaps the best formula for a successful bed and breakfast; it gives the guest a refuge from the cares and problems of home — while at the same time replicating (or at least simulating) a feeling of "at-homeness."

There are two parts, or phases, to Elk Cove Inn. One is the main house, where Michael and Hildrun live. Here are two guest rooms; guests sit in the evening by the fire to hear the Boynoffs' huge collection of classical music. Most guests find themselves in Sandpiper House, an annex originally built for visitors to the lumber company. It is about half a mile away.

Sandpiper House is flanked by handsome camellia trees. There is a large redwood-paneled common room, again with a brick fireplace. My favorite room is No. 3, featuring a view of the ocean that took my breath away. (The old-fashioned flowered-wallpaper design and slightly campy potted palm were just right for this room.) Paths lead from both houses to private, secluded beaches.

Breakfast here is a delight. Hildrun is well known for her German egg cakes (Eierkuchen) with freshly picked blackberries or huckleberries, coffee, and orange juice. For dinner you might be served Königsberger Klops (poached meatballs in lemon-caper sauce), Sauer-braten, Rouladen, Hasenpfeffer (rabbit in a sour cream sauce) — or any number of excellent French dishes.

Green Dolphin Inn

6145 South Highway One
Elk, California 95432; (707) 877-3342

INNKEEPERS:	Bill Reed and Elaine Beldin.
ACCOMMODATIONS:	Three rooms, all with private bath; two queen-size and one king-size bed.
RESERVATIONS:	Three weeks recommended.
MINIMUM STAY:	Two nights.
DEPOSIT:	First night's lodging.
CREDIT CARDS:	MC, VISA.
RATES:	Moderate.
RESTRICTIONS:	No children. No pets.

I liked this unpretentious, very comfortable bed and breakfast as much for the people who are the hosts as for the environment it provides. The cozy interiors are a delight, but the sincere and unaffected enthusiasm of proprietors Bill Reed and Elaine Beldin is the main attraction here. I'm apparently not the only person who feels this way; a solid majority of the guests at any time represents repeat business.

Bill Reed was a bookkeeper before he was an inn-keeper; Elaine Beldin was a legislative secretary in Sacramento. When midlife crisis made its inevitable appearance, the two friends decided to confront it together. They had always liked this part of the California coastline, so when the chance presented itself, they took the plunge into the uncertain waters of the bed and breakfast business.

I'm glad they did. The heavily beamed, spacious Commons Room contains one of the most massive fireplaces I've seen. Books in the library lean heavily toward the classics; there are also games and a color TV for those whose taste runs to less introspective amusements. But it was the cheerful warmth of Bill and Elaine that impressed me most. Their pride in their establishment was obvious as they showed me the rest of their accommodations.

The kitchen and dining room are on the second

floor, offering what Elaine unabashedly refers to as "a truly magnificent view." The dining room has a fireplace, and there is a small balcony directly adjacent to it. (There is also a small sitting area on the second floor.) The single bedroom on this level sports a very large and somewhat Gothic-looking wood stove. The other two bedrooms are in the Carriage House in back, with a deck and a hot tub nearby. All rooms contain antiques, many of which are for sale.

The thing for which the Green Dolphin is perhaps best known (besides the friendliness of its proprietors) is its hearty breakfast. The bill of fare changes regularly, but the one unalterable house rule is that no one goes away hungry. This very American all-you-can-eat policy contrasts markedly with the Continental breakfast. "People like to feel special," Elaine says, "and I simply enjoy making them feel that way."

Navarro Ridge Inn

33810 Navarro Ridge Road
Albion, California 95410; (707) 937-4511

INNKEEPER:	*Terry Alt.*
ACCOMMODATIONS:	*Nine rooms and one large cottage; queen-size beds.*
RESERVATIONS:	*Three weeks.*
MINIMUM STAY:	*Two nights on weekends.*
DEPOSIT:	*$25.*
CREDIT CARDS:	*Not accepted.*
RATES:	*Inexpensive to moderate.*
RESTRICTIONS:	*Children in cottage only. No pets.*

T his inn offers nineteen acres of unspoiled coastal countryside for its lucky guests to unwind in. There are also bicycles for the use of the guests in their exploration of the coastal roads, and darkroom facilities are available for photographers. These are only a few of the extras of this very reasonably priced establishment that has been open just since July 4, 1980.

The Navarro's history dates back to the 1860s (though it may have been built even earlier) when it was a way station for lumbermen and other travelers on the coast. Between 1883 and 1894 it was an official Wells Fargo inn, offering food, drink, and lodging. Around the turn of the century the tavern was added to the main house; it was well known as a raucous place "unfit for ladies." The Alts have restored it to the warm and rustic style of its Victorian days. The key word here is *rustic* — it is the most "country" of all the Mendocino inns I toured.

Terry Alt came to Mendocino County in 1979 for the Mendocino Art Center program in textiles. She had already remodeled an older home in Mill Valley, and the innkeeping idea had been in the back of her mind for some time. When she saw a real estate sign in front of this old dwelling, she instantly knew what she wanted it to look like; and the rest (as they say in the hostelry trade) was all hard work.

Opening night was July 4, 1980 — and what a night! There was a fire, and the phone went out. In fact the telephone didn't come back on for four months. Then the Navarro was closed by the county for more work to meet the building codes, which are very strictly enforced around these parts. "I'm just now getting back on my feet," Terry says.

The furniture here is Early American, which for me enhances rather than conflicts with the Victorian lines of the house. There is a fireplace and a spinning wheel in the Old Tavern. There is a library for those for whom reading is the best relaxation. Guests may use the phonograph in the library, as well as the many games and puzzles.

All bedrooms have cast-iron stoves or fireplaces, and handmade quilts. I liked the Attic Suite best. This is a very private hideaway with a private bath, a brick fireplace, and a canopied bed; and there's a second bedroom with French doors, for those big entrances you've always dreamed about but never made.

Breakfast is leisurely but substantial: French toast, fresh fruit compote, melon balls, coffee cake, cheese omelettes, coffee, and tea. There is usually music, from chamber to bluegrass, on Saturday nights and Sunday afternoons. (The Alts are confirmed fans of country and folk.)

This inn is just too good not to succeed in a big way. It is another of those places you should visit *now,* before the mobs arrive.

Victorian Farmhouse

7001 North Highway One
Little River, California 95456; (707) 937-0697

INNKEEPERS:	*Thomas and Jane Szilasi.*
ACCOMMODATIONS:	*Four rooms, all with private bath; three queen- and one king-size bed.*
RESERVATIONS:	*Three to four weeks recommended.*
MINIMUM STAY:	*Two nights on weekends, April through October.*
DEPOSIT:	*First night's lodging.*
CREDIT CARDS:	*MC, VISA.*
RATES:	*Moderate.*
RESTRICTIONS:	*No children under sixteen. No pets.*

I t was built in 1877 by John and Emma Dora Dennen as a private residence, which it still is. A pronounced feeling of privacy is the most striking attribute of this homey inn. But a certain atmosphere of permanence — of stability — runs it a close second. One doesn't visit here so much as reside, even if the duration of that residence is only a week or a weekend.

Thomas Szilasi was once a pharmaceutical salesman; his wife Jane was a stewardess for TWA. They lived in the sprawling, ever-growing metropolis of San Jose. One day they sat down and wrote a list of all the things they liked, as well as the things they didn't. (A wise and provident couple, these two.) Bed and breakfast inns were close to the top of their list of likable things, so when this property was listed in the *Wall Street Journal* they decided to settle down with an inn of their own.

Then came the hard work. Tom did the "nail-bending" part of the restoration; Jane was and is the master decorator. Both gloried in the lack of neon signs, stoplights, and billboards in Little River. "It's nice to get back to basics," says Tom. "I enjoy taking people at their word, trusting people." It's something that seems to happen more in the country than the city, they feel.

They also feel that their inn is ideal for traveling couples. There are several acres — and an orchard of apple, plum, and pear — to ramble around in. I liked the solid triple-hung bay windows in the downstairs parlor, and the Regulator clock, and the fireplace; both upstairs rooms have ocean views, while one downstairs has a French wood-burning stove and its own sitting room. (The other has an exquisite view of a small private flower garden.)

A queen-size brass bed graces the Emma Dora room; there are white comforters and pillow shams, and a ceiling done in a tasteful (and restful) redwood design. I also liked the upstairs sitting room with its small desk overlooking both the beach and the garden.

Breakfast comes a few minutes after 8:00 — guests are served in their rooms. (Bran and raisin muffins, peach yogurt with sliced bananas and granola, fresh OJ, and coffee, tea, or hot chocolate.) Other typical morning dishes are croissants, apple juice, and fresh fruit in season. Sometimes guests are served fruit fresh from the orchard outside.

Whatever you eat in the morning, the fresh ocean breeze in these parts will make it taste better than anything you could eat in the city. The quiet pace and restful environment of this inn is most conducive to concentration and creativity — an excellent place to sort out one's thoughts and prepare emotionally for that big project back in the workaday world.

Glendeven

8221 North Highway One
Little River, California 95456; (707) 937-0083

INNKEEPERS:	*Jan and Janet DeVries.*
ACCOMMODATIONS:	*Seven rooms, three with private bath; double and queen-size beds.*
RESERVATIONS:	*Six weeks for weekends; two weeks Monday through Thursday.*
MINIMUM STAY:	*Two nights on weekends.*
DEPOSIT:	*First night's lodging.*
CREDIT CARDS:	*Not accepted.*
RATES:	*Moderate to expensive.*
RESTRICTIONS:	*No children under six. No pets.*

G lendeven was the country home of Isaiah Stevens, who moved here with a group of settlers from Maine. He raised and bred fine horses and cattle on his one-hundred-acre farm — and also built a farmhouse in 1867 for his bride, Rebecca Coombs. It was and is a distinctly New England-looking house, typical of the architecture in the Mendocino area; many of the early settlers were from that region.

In the 1950s the house was bought by Warren and Dora Zimmer, who began its restoration. Jan DeVries, who was then a student, saw it during a visit to the coast in 1962. He returned later as a teacher, and married Janet Bell — and the couple promptly left for Portland. But the rugged north coast (and perhaps the romance associated with their courtship) continued to exert its pull. When the DeVrieses heard of the impending sale of the Zimmer house, they returned (in 1977) to open it as an inn.

This is the perfect place to get over a bad case of office politics, a disappointment in love, or the kind of blahs associated with the morning headlines. The dominant note here is upbeat. Antique furnishings sit side by side with modern pieces, ceramics, and works of art; colorful, cheery abstract paintings hang on the walls. The

effect is quite consciously calculated to elevate the mood. And it succeeds admirably.

My favorite rooms are the Garret, a surprisingly large attic room with dormers, tucked under the eaves of the roof (with a rocking chair and a writing desk); and the Garden Room with its armoire, large hanging plants, and country-meadow atmosphere. Guests in both rooms receive breakfast on a tray. The DeVrieses say that breakfast is "somewhere in between" full and Continental: bread or muffins, coffee cake, croissants, cold-hard-cooked eggs, juice, and a variety of fresh fruits — including, if you are lucky, their tasty red apples.

Exploring the parlor, I discovered a grand piano and a row of large-paned windows looking out on the grounds, which contain several bright gardens. The light and airy feeling was enhanced by the large red barn in back (in which the DeVrieses are now building their own living quarters) and the lovely cypress trees that flank and surround both structures.

Not far from Glendeven the forest begins. But it is not Robert Frost's "lovely, dark, and deep" New England woods. Rather it is a place of laughter, a certain youthful playfulness, and the bright colors of an uncomplicated childhood. Again it is Frost who expresses this sense of childlike play: "So was I once a swinger of birches. And so I dream of going back to be."

Headlands Inn

44950 Albion Street
Mendocino, California 95460; (707) 937-4431

INNKEEPERS:	*Lynn Anderson, Pete Albrecht, Kathy and John Casper.*
ACCOMMODATIONS:	*Five rooms, all with private bath; queen and king-size beds.*
RESERVATIONS:	*Four weeks recommended.*
MINIMUM STAY:	*Two nights on weekends.*
DEPOSIT:	*First night's lodging.*
CREDIT CARDS:	*Not accepted.*
RATES:	*Inexpensive to moderate.*
RESTRICTIONS:	*No children. No pets.*

The Headlands Inn began as a barbershop on Main Street in the town of Mendocino in 1868. Five years later a second story was added for the barber and his family. Afterwards the dwelling was used as a saloon, a hotel annex, and a private residence. In 1883 it was moved to its present location at Howard and Albion streets. Bessie Strauss and her husband John bought the house in 1924; renovation was completed in 1979.

The building was already an inn when John and Kathy Casper found that it was up for sale (they lived three miles up the road). At that time Peter Albrecht and Lynn Anderson were living in the Virgin Islands; they longed to settle in the Pacific Northwest. The four entrepreneurs got together and formed a partnership, and are now collectively the owner-operators of the Headlands.

The dwelling is three stories high, with clean, solid lines — most definitely a Victorian with a New England character. The modern conveniences are not lacking; all five rooms have private bathrooms, and three have fireplaces. Two are attic rooms with window seats, the best view of the town I saw while I was there. (Look particularly for Mendocino's quaint water towers.) Certain rooms come with a private balcony.

My favorite room is No. 2: bay windows facing the

ocean, a redwood fireplace, a large mirrored armoire, a rocking chair, lace curtains — and a wonderful king-size bed truly fit for a king.

Breakfast is fresh-baked breads and muffins, freshly squeezed orange juice or fresh fruit, coffee and tea. It arrives on a breakfast tray with fresh flowers. (The day I was there a delicious lemon bread was part of the morning menu.)

Local attractions are many and varied. There is an art center, secluded sandy beaches, tide pools teeming with marine life, hiking (three state parks are within ten miles of Mendocino), golfing, and canoeing on Big River. But for many, simply walking through Mendocino is enough: it bears an astonishing resemblance to a New England fishing village and has been used as a backdrop for Hollywood productions. There are many fine restaurants in the area; complimentary wine is served in the afternoon at the Headlands.

Joshua Grindle Inn

44800 Little Lake
Mendocino, California 95460; (707) 937-4143

INNKEEPERS:	*Gwen and Bill Jacobson.*
ACCOMMODATIONS:	*Seven rooms, all with private bath; twin, double, and king-size beds.*
RESERVATIONS:	*Ten to twelve weeks.*
MINIMUM STAY:	*None.*
DEPOSIT:	*First night's lodging.*
CREDIT CARDS:	*Not accepted.*
RATES:	*Inexpensive to moderate.*
RESTRICTIONS:	*Children discouraged. No pets.*

L
ike so many others, the Grindle clan had come to the North Coast from Maine. This lovely Italianate home was built as a wedding present on the marriage of Joshua Grindle and Alice Hills, in 1879 — a gift from the bride's father. Alice died in childbirth in 1882, but the house remained in the Grindle family until 1967. In 1977 Bill and Gwen Jacobson bought the house and turned it into a first-class inn.

The Jacobsons have so enhanced the "back east" tone of this intricate bed and breakfast that it can stand up to the very best New England establishment. And it is a very romantic place; a natural, I would think, for a honeymoon.

The first things I noticed on entering were the Early American pieces in the parlor (along with the fireplace and grand piano). Colonial-era furnishings appear extensively throughout the rest of the house. (All guest rooms have handmade quilts from New England.) The Library Room has an old-fashioned four-poster and fine hand-crafted cabinets and shelves. In the dining room I found a harvest table seating ten, and Pennsylvania Dutch-style wallpaper. Impeccable taste and cleanliness add to the eastern feeling.

In back there is a cottage with two rooms, a Frank-

lin fireplace, wood-beamed ceilings, and a large bath. (Both rooms are accessible by wheelchair.)

The Grindle has a good collection of old clocks that will remind you pleasantly of all the time you have to fritter away. I also liked the extensive collection of etchings, oil paintings, and serigraphs. Two of the guest rooms have fireplaces decorated with hand-crafted tiles done in 1870 at Ninton's, Stoke on Trent, a factory in England. (The tiles in the Library Room illustrate *Aesop's Fables*.)

Although Gwen serves a Continental breakfast, it sometimes includes eggs from a nearby farm. The usual fare consists of fruit with coffee cake, huckleberry muffins, popovers, homemade bread, tea and coffee. There are always apples and oranges in the parlor for guests, as well as a decanter of sherry. And bicycles are available to guests for exploring this most interesting of little coastal enclaves.

Whitegate Inn

499 Howard Street
Mendocino, California 95460; (707) 937-4892

INNKEEPERS:	*Robbie and Wally Clegg.*
ACCOMMODATIONS:	*Six rooms, four with private bath; twin, double, and queen-size beds.*
RESERVATIONS:	*Three to four weeks recommended.*
MINIMUM STAY:	*Two nights on weekends.*
DEPOSIT:	*First night's lodging.*
CREDIT CARDS:	*Not accepted.*
RATES:	*Inexpensive to moderate.*
RESTRICTIONS:	*Children discouraged. No pets.*

T his house was built in 1880 by Dr. William McCornack, a local physician. He used it as his hospital, and it retained its healing-arts association well into living memory; it was called the McCornack Healing Center before its purchase by Bill Reed and Elaine Beldin (now owners of the Green Dolphin Inn in Elk). Robbie and Wally Clegg finished the restoration begun by Bill and Elaine — exactly one hundred years after the inn was built.

Many things have changed in the last hundred years, but not the service orientation of the building's succession of owners. Robbie enjoys serving people; in fact, she feels people don't ask for enough. "It's as though they want to be imposed upon — or think they'll be imposing on *us* if they ask for something." Don't feel that way when you visit Whitegate. Your hosts will not only be two of the youngest innkeepers I have encountered (they are both in their early thirties), but among the most enthusiastic. Their innkeeping style includes spending as much time as possible with guests and acting as their guides through the north coast panorama.

Wally and Robbie lived in Marin County before moving to Mendocino. She worked as a bartender (now *there's* a serving profession for you!); Wally was in the computer business. Both had stayed at bed and breakfast inns in northern California and the Pacific Northwest. They heard about the McCornack house through Mendocino's real estate grapevine, and, after purchasing it, filled it with pieces once possessed by former owners, antiques with a local history, and a few special family heirlooms.

The house is well appointed, with gilt ceiling moldings and plaster medallions; the parlor contains two Victorian settees, a grand Hamilton pump organ, lots of green plants, a stereo system, and a good collection of local-interest books for those curious about the area. Breakfast is served in the parlor, as is wine in the afternoon.

The morning meal is a generous one: a full breakfast is served on the weekends (featuring excellent banana-nut waffles when I stayed here — the Cleggs are noted for the variety of waffles they serve); weekdays guests receive a Continental breakfast of nut breads with cream cheese and flavored butters, fresh fruit, coffee, and tea.

I slept in the Cypress Room: bay windows, a beautiful red-dragon design Oriental carpet, an armoire, white lace curtains with a white eyelet down comforter and pillow shams. This room has its own bath and is sheltered by a lovely cypress tree.

Robbie tells with pleasure of the guests who were married at the nearby Headlands Inn and stayed the night at the Whitegate. (Robbie and Wally were their witnesses.) They're also proud of a recent marriage proposal made here. As well they might be. One could do worse than begin a marriage at this pretty and reasonably priced inn. And I cannot think of better witnesses at a wedding ceremony than this energetic, winsome, and very solicitous couple.

Country Inn

632 North Main Street
Fort Bragg, California 95437; (707) 964-3737

INNKEEPERS:	*Don and Helen Miller.*
ACCOMMODATIONS:	*Eight rooms, all with private bath; seven queen- and one king-size bed.*
RESERVATIONS:	*Two to three weeks recommended.*
MINIMUM STAY:	*None.*
DEPOSIT:	*First night's lodging.*
CREDIT CARDS:	*MC, VISA.*
RATES:	*Inexpensive.*
RESTRICTIONS:	*No children. No pets.*

We may never know for whom this charming structure was built, but we do know it belonged to the Union Lumber Company. In 1893 it was sold to a Mr. L. A. Moody for $500 — a princely sum in those days. (A 1905 edition of the *San Francisco Examiner* found glued to the redwood wallboards here advertises overalls at the bargain price of 17¢ each.)

The building has passed through many hands (and lives) since then. In 1975 Don and Helen Miller moved to Fort Bragg on the craggy Mendocino County coast. Don was working as a free-lance writer, photographer, artisan, and sculptor (he calls himself a one-man advertising agency). He found himself doing a volume business writing and designing brochures for local innkeepers. It occurred to the couple that owning their own bed and breakfast inn would be an ideal way to meet people. And so it has been. (It has also given Helen a chance to pursue one of her favorite avocations: baking bread.)

This is not one of those bed and breakfasts where one is forever afraid to touch anything for fear it might break. Not that the Millers sacrifice the personal touch. Country Inn is appointed throughout with Don's photographs, sculpture, and watercolors. (The skylight in the parlor not only creates excellent light with which to view them, but accentuates the feeling of comfort and relaxa-

tion.) I liked the redwood banisters on the stairway and the carefully chosen wallpaper; the exterior is entirely done in redwood paneling.

Each of the bedrooms has plush carpeting, and wallpaper is coordinated with sheets and pillowcases. All of the bathrooms are modern (the attic bedroom has a claw-foot tub, however); one is accessible by wheelchair with special facilities for the handicapped.

Helen makes four delicious varieties of nut and fruit breads (blackberry, banana, lemon, and orange). Breakfast also includes melon wedges and slices of other fruits in season, and coffee and orange juice.

Nearby attractions are surprisingly varied in Fort Bragg (a "one-taxi" town). The Footlighter Theater produces locally written musical comedy (usually old-fashioned melodramas in which the audience is encouraged to cheer the fair-haired hero, and the villain makes his entrance to boos and hisses). It runs May through August. Fort Bragg is also noted for its many shops and art galleries, gardens, museums — and its award-winning gourmet ice cream.

Don and Helen speak fondly of the couple who were the first to share their accommodations. "We were mortified to find out later that the bathtub had no plug," Don told me. But the Millers needn't have worried — two weeks later their guests sent them a bottle of wine.

I'm not surprised. Making the great escape into total relaxation is not easy to achieve, but the congenial Millers have a formula that works.

Pudding Creek Inn

700 North Main Street
Fort Bragg, California 95437; (707) 964-9529

INNKEEPERS:	*Marilyn and Gene Gundersen.*
ACCOMMODATIONS:	*Twelve rooms, all with private bath; twin, double, queen- and king-size beds.*
RESERVATIONS:	*Two to three weeks recommended.*
MINIMUM STAY:	*Two nights over holidays.*
DEPOSIT:	*First night's lodging.*
CREDIT CARDS:	*VISA.*
RATES:	*Inexpensive.*
RESTRICTIONS:	*No children under twelve. No pets.*

This very pretty Victorian was built in 1884 by a Russian count who fled the Old World under a cloud. He did not arrive in the New penniless, however; some people were even so uncharitable as to suggest that he had departed with money that was not, legally speaking, his own. Ill-gotten or not, he put his spoils to good use, building seven fine homes in the Fort Bragg area.

In deference to the democratic traditions of his new homeland (and fear of the Russian authorities, probably) our hero changed his name to the less aristocratic — and considerably more anonymous — appellation of Mr. Brown. His wedding was the occasion of considerable local interest: his bride wore the first wedding dress advertised in the Montgomery Ward catalog.

Records reveal that an equally anonymous Mr. Woods and Mrs. White later owned and lived in the count's aging home. In the 1970s it was rescued by Marilyn and Gene Gundersen and restored; in August 1980 it opened as a bed and breakfast inn, its hallways presided over by pictures of the count and his wife.

Actually there are two dwellings; both are connected by an enclosed garden court. (Breakfast is served here in the summer, and in the antique store—kitchen during winter.) Breakfast consists of juice, fresh fruit, homemade coffee cakes, and coffee or tea. If it is warm weather and you eat outside, you can enjoy the many varieties of fuchsias, begonias, and ferns in the garden court. (Complimentary wine is also served here from 5:00 to 6:00 P.M.)

As we go to press there are a total of twelve guest rooms. The Spinning Room is done in yellow and blue, with a queen-size bed. (There's an additional bunk bed and a private bath directly across the hall.) My favorite is the Interlude Room. Shades of Cole Porter's *Blue Room:* everything is blue here (including baby blue), with priscilla curtains. The king-size bed is pecan wood, and there is a spacious bathroom. Altogether a light, sunny and very romantic room that I highly recommend.

A small country store is located in the downstairs of one of the dwellings for your browsing enjoyment. It has collectibles, antiques, and gifts. There are many shops and restaurants nearby, and tennis courts are available a few blocks away. There is a Visitors' Center in town to familiarize those who are passing through with the many activities in the community.

This inn is a favorite of at least one well-known character actress. It could become your favorite too. I'm sure the roguish old count who sought refuge in the far reaches of the New World would relish the quiet good taste here — and who could help but applaud the very democratic prices associated with this modern incarnation of his nineteenth-century hideaway?

The Grey Whale Inn

615 North Main Street
Fort Bragg, California 95437; (707) 964-0640

INNKEEPERS:	*John and Colette Bailey.*
ACCOMMODATIONS:	*Thirteen rooms, eleven with private bath; twin, double, queen- and king-size beds.*
RESERVATIONS:	*Three weeks for weekends.*
MINIMUM STAY:	*Two nights over holidays.*
DEPOSIT:	*First night's lodging.*
CREDIT CARDS:	*AE, MC, VISA.*
RATES:	*Inexpensive to moderate.*
RESTRICTIONS:	*No pets (local kennel accommodations).*

F ort Bragg's first (and perhaps its most distinctive) bed and breakfast inn, the Grey Whale, features spacious, comfortable rooms — most with private bath — at very affordable prices. This is an extremely interesting establishment for several different reasons, not the least of which is the discriminating staff. I found a genuine desire to please here, and considerable knowledge about the Fort Bragg area of Mendocino County.

The building itself has long been a landmark, having served from 1915, when it was built, until 1971 as the Redwood Coast Hospital, the north coast's major health facility. The weathered redwood siding, completely covering the white clapboard, is trimmed with fresh colors. As more than one observer has noted, it looks as though it had always been an inn — a testament to the skill of those who designed the conversion.

John Bailey worked for Alpha Beta markets, Colette at a Veterans Hospital; both wished to do something for themselves. They spent a year looking in northern California before they found the right place. (It was advertised in the *Wall Street Journal*.) John enjoys dealing with people in a cooperative, rather than a competitive, way. "One gets positive feedback," Colette says. "The corporate world is a long way from Fort Bragg."

There is a wide variety of rooms here, in terms of size, decor, and views. Hallways are spacious, stairs are easy (guest rooms are on three levels); one bedroom and bath contains accommodations for the handicapped, including ramp access. The Baileys' private collection of art works is displayed throughout the building, with a strong emphasis on work by local artists. (The magnificent whale on the front grounds was carved by Byrd Baker, a leader in the Save the Whales movement.)

Guests are encouraged to let the staff know in advance of special requirements regarding food. Breakfast is served from 7:30 to 11:00 A.M. every morning in the Breakfast Room. It includes homemade fruit or nut breads or coffee cake, fresh fruit, juice, and hot drinks. (Guests can take breakfast to their room on trays.)

Guests interested in local activities are supplied with a big book of things to do in the area, easily the most extensive and helpful that I saw during my tour. There are a surprising number of attractions: Noyo Harbor with its fishing fleet, state parks and beaches, redwood forests galore, art galleries, concerts, and even good local opera at certain times of the year. (Annual town festivals include a salmon barbecue in July and Paul Bunyan Days in the fall.)

John and Colette recount as their most interesting experience the time a gentleman and his companion took two of the Grey Whale's towels. No police reports, threats, or tense letters with the names of lawyers on the letterhead; the Baileys simply wrote and asked politely for the return of the towels. A week later they arrived — along with a very chastened note of apology. Who says nice guys always finish last?

One of the most successful bed and breakfast inns I visited, this, and it is easy to see why. It does something that many inns aim for but do not always achieve: it affords the *joie de vivre* of many people gathered under one roof in pleasant surroundings — yet still succeeds, through its conscientious attention to the needs and preferences of the individual, in making each guest feel special.

The Blue Rose Inn

520 North Main Street
Fort Bragg, California 95437; (707) 964-3477

INNKEEPER:	*Anne Samas.*
ACCOMMODATIONS:	*Five rooms, four with private bath; double and queen-size beds.*
RESERVATIONS:	*One month recommended.*
MINIMUM STAY:	*None.*
DEPOSIT:	*First night's lodging.*
CREDIT CARDS:	*Not accepted.*
RATES:	*Moderate.*
RESTRICTIONS:	*No children. No pets.*

A nne Samas was raised in southwestern Penn-sylvania, and she remembers clearly the popu-larity of the "guest house." (Motels were once referred to in this part of the country as "motorhotels.") The guest house — or tourist home, as it was sometimes called — was usually a private residence with one or more rooms available to the traveler in search of more personal (and probably less expensive) lodging. Add the break-fast — which many guest houses in Pennsylvania tradi-tionally served — and you have the classic bed and breakfast experience as one generally finds it in Europe and the British Isles.

Anne came to Mendocino in 1962, planning to open a tourist home herself. She priced several houses, but none seemed right. It was not until 1976 that she bought the present structure. It is a ninety-five-year-old Cape Cod Victorian, and she and her son David have done wonders with it. Her plant-filled establishment is enhanced by redwood ceilings, Tiffany and crystal chan-deliers, and attractive wallpaper patterns imported from Korea, Japan, and France.

This is definitely a bed and breakfast inn rather than a private home offering bed and breakfast accommo-dations, but it exhibits much of the informality of a guest house. Anne's living quarters are in the rear, in an old shed she and David have transformed into a very nice little cottage. She feels this gives guests more elbow room. "Since I'm not technically on the premises, they can do whatever they want," she says. "They have the run of the kitchen and can use the refrigerator, for example." She adds: "When a guest first arrives, I spend some time with him. After that, I'm available — but I don't get in the way."

The rooms — like Anne's garden, which she modestly calls "the best garden in Fort Bragg" — are brightly hued in colors calculated to refresh as well as relax. I liked the French Provincial, which follows a color scheme of gold and lavender. The Blue Room is blue and off-white, with an antique bed of walnut, a marble-topped dresser and washstand, and a claw-foot tub in the bath. (Guests relax in the Green Room, the kitchen, and the parlor — the last-named contains rattan chairs from Taiwan and a fine hand-carved screen.)

Anne is of the opinion that when leaving the toil and turmoil of city life and the working world, one should not continue to punch the time clock. So there is no set time for breakfast: it begins at 8:00 and continues until everybody has finished. Anne sets out quiche, cinnamon-raisin bread, fruit in season, orange juice, milk, and tea and coffee. Guests are supplied with bacon and eggs, which they can make for themselves any time they feel ready for breakfast.

This distinctive laissez-faire policy is also in effect concerning one's departure. The Blue Rose has no check-out time. "Many times guests will still be sitting around the kitchen table talking with other guests over breakfast until noon or even later," Anne says. She makes it clear that this informality is one of the things that make her accommodations friendlier and more relaxed than most — and I heartily agree.

Glass Beach Inn

726 North Main Street
Fort Bragg, California 95437; (707) 964-6774

INNKEEPERS:	*Robert and Beverly Sallinen.*
ACCOMMODATIONS:	*Four rooms, all with private bath; double and queen-size beds.*
RESERVATIONS:	*Two weeks recommended.*
MINIMUM STAY:	*None.*
DEPOSIT:	*Full amount.*
CREDIT CARDS:	*Not accepted.*
RATES:	*Moderate.*
RESTRICTIONS:	*Children discouraged. No pets.*

Glass Beach Inn's proprietor, Robert Sallinen, tells of the guest who demanded his money back on arrival. "I told him I was sorry. At breakfast the next day he said he would like to stay a second day." As I see it his change of heart must have been due to one (or perhaps both) of two reasons: a very hearty full breakfast (sausage, bacon or ham, eggs, pancakes, fruits and fruit juices served buffet style, breads or muffins, and coffee or tea); and a totally private (and very relaxing) hot tub available to guests on a "sign up" system.

Guest rooms include the Oriental Jade room, with antique satin and Oriental figurine lamps (wife Beverly is responsible for the interior decoration). The bed is an old-fashioned four-poster; there is a large fireplace to add warmth to your evening. The Victorian Rose features rich, red velvet on the Edwardian double bed, and handsome marble-topped tables.

I opt for Country Comfort, quiet, quaint, and intimate. (Old trunks and rockers, an armoire, a cozy Franklin fireplace, dark blue wallpaper and white lace.) Second choice is Malaysian Experience: cheerful, spacious, and sunny. Wicker furniture and fan-backed chairs add to the Asian atmosphere here.

The Sallinens have just opened two new rooms. Grandma's Attic is now the largest in the house. The Schooner Mendocino is the most whimsical: beaded glass windows flanked by dormers, and a bed hanging from ropes attached to the ceiling.

Glass Beach Inn is close to the beach, as well as to the famous Skunk Train. This is an old-fashioned railroad train that takes its passengers deep into the redwood country east of town. There is a half-day trip, as well as a full day's excursion for the more energetic. Beverly and Robert (or Pam Sallinen, the resident manager) will be happy to help you make reservations.

Cobweb Palace Inn

38921 North Highway One
Westport, California 95488; (707) 964-5588

INNKEEPERS:	*Dave Cantley and Peter Husk.*
ACCOMMODATIONS:	*Six rooms, four with private bath; double and queen-size beds.*
RESERVATIONS:	*Three to four weeks recommended.*
MINIMUM STAY:	*Two nights over holidays.*
DEPOSIT:	*First night's lodging plus half of additional nights.*
CREDIT CARDS:	*AE, MC, VISA.*
RATES:	*Inexpensive.*
RESTRICTIONS:	*No children. No pets.*

Westport is a community of some eighty souls on the Mendocino coast. Ask anyone what to do in Westport, and the answer you'll get is "nothing." Some say that Westport now offers what the town of Mendocino used to: peace and quiet in an environment of near-total isolation. (That is, free of tourists.) And to be sure, Westport does in many ways resemble a much smaller Mendocino, or perhaps the Mendocino of an earlier time.

In keeping with the theme of peaceful isolation, the two innkeepers of the Cobweb Palace follow an enlightened laissez-faire policy toward guests. "We try to leave our guests alone," says Peter, "but without ignoring them." The proprietors complement each other well: if Peter is the more energetic of the pair, Dave is the calm in the eye of the storm. He's originally from Nova Scotia, so this area feels very much like home to him.

It was Dave who found the building. On March 1, 1979 he was an accountant living in Laguna Beach. (Peter was a high school teacher.) He was just about to throw away a newspaper when he felt a "prickly feeling" in his thumb. He looked under it and saw an ad for the sale of a "Victorian Western hotel." The two friends flew up to take a look; it was a building more than one hundred years old. A short time later both were in the bed and breakfast inn business.

A true Western Victorian, it has a false front with boardwalks. It was a hotel originally owned by a local lumber company in the nineteenth century; afterwards it was successively a private residence and a bordello — and finally a hangout of the flower children of the 1960s. It has now been restored to its original glory, in what its new owners call "country comfortable." (The Cobweb Palace's exterior is now painted pewter and dusty coral, accented with white trim.)

A surprisingly homelike atmosphere is encountered within. The Gold Room has a queen-size bed, two comfortable overstuffed rocking chairs, and contemporary furnishings. The Green Room has a sofa and chair in a small sitting area. (Both rooms have a private bath and balcony, overlooking the ocean.) Light gray with pale-pink trim enhances the charm and brightness of other interiors.

Breakfast is fruit compote, muffins (apple, pear, and blueberry), homemade preserves (Dave is the proud creator of these), OJ, and coffee, tea, or hot chocolate. (A full breakfast can be had if ordered in advance — there is a slight extra charge for it.) Breakfast is taken in the bar area from 8:00 to 9:00 weekdays and Saturdays, between 9:00 and 10:00 Sundays.

Cobweb Palace has no TV. Its proud and exacting new owners explain its absence in the following way:

> Two things we have for viewing
> That quite surpass TV
> In color, sound and drama:
> Log fires, and the sea.

DeHaven Valley Farm

North Highway One, P.O. Box 128
Westport, California 95488; (707) 964-2931

INNKEEPERS:	*Tina Ginnelli and Gale Fairbrother.*
ACCOMMODATIONS:	*Six rooms and a cottage, all with shared bath; one suite with private bath; twin, double, queen- and king-size beds.*
RESERVATIONS:	*Three to four weeks recommended.*
MINIMUM STAY:	*Two nights over holidays.*
DEPOSIT:	*First night's lodging.*
CREDIT CARDS:	*AE, MC, VISA.*
RATES:	*Inexpensive to moderate.*
RESTRICTIONS:	*Children discouraged. No pets (local kennel arrangements).*

T his classic late-1880s Victorian country home was the brainchild of a wealthy businessman who had made his fortune in the lumber industry. Alexander Gordon, a Canadian born in Montreal, was originally associated with the Kelley and Rundle sawmill in nearby Westport; in 1875 he bought one thousand acres of ranch land and became a cattleman, selling beef to the logging camps. (His total holdings here once amounted to seven thousand acres.) Before moving on to Ventura County in southern California he built this lovely rambling home, one of the nicest hideaways you will find on the bed and breakfast circuit.

This is real seclusion. (The closest town is tiny Westport, with only two hundred residents.) Its forty acres include hiking trails, a beach, lush pine forests, and a fresh-water stream. But the DeHaven is also a working farm. Sheep and cows abound — as well as horses for riding. All vegetables served here come from the farm's garden.

Gale Fairbrother worked in executive personnel placement before coming to Mendocino County. She had been coming to the north coast for many years but hadn't figured out a way to make a living here. Tina Ginnelli had owned a real estate investment firm and was looking for a place to spend her weekends. The pair met through a mutual friend and decided that what they really ought to do was open an inn or guest ranch. They found the old DeHaven Valley farmhouse, and in May 1981 opened it as a bed and breakfast inn.

Some of the rooms feature antique beds (iron, wicker, and brass) with handmade throws. Small antique bureaus, mirrors, and lamps are also the rule (including some oil lamps), set off by attractive Cape Cod curtains. The parlor has a large brick fireplace and a well-stocked library ranging from the classics to the merely entertaining. In the dining room are handsome oak tables and chairs, with cut-glass and crystal chandeliers with hand-painted roses. (The entire house is newly carpeted.)

Of the guest accommodations, the Red Room is one of the most striking: red and white wallpaper, an iron bed, a white down comforter trimmed with eyelet lace, and an antique white bowl and pitcher. The DeHaven Suite contains a king-size bed and a Franklin stove, a wide-beamed ceiling, and a private bath under the eaves.

Breakfast is homemade muffins, freshly squeezed OJ, a fresh fruit salad bowl (one of the nicest I've seen), and tea or the house blend of coffee (Colombian and French roast). It is served between 9:00 and 10:00; guests may take their food wherever they feel most comfortable. (The parlor opens onto a deck with a picnic table and chairs.) Gourmet dinners are also served here at reasonable prices, and a champagne breakfast in bed can be arranged for only the cost of the bubbly.

This restful country retreat has known a number of different proprietors in the last few years, probably the best known of which would be Jim and Rachel Sears, who did the original renovation. It's nice to see that the new team has not only retained but has enhanced the charm achieved by the DeHaven Valley Farm's former owners.

Howard Creek Ranch

North Highway One, P.O. Box 121
Westport, California 95488; (707) 964-6725

INNKEEPERS:	*Sunny and Sally Lasselle.*
ACCOMMODATIONS:	*Seven rooms with shared baths; double beds.*
RESERVATIONS:	*One week recommended.*
MINIMUM STAY:	*None.*
DEPOSIT:	*None required.*
CREDIT CARDS:	*Not accepted.*
RATES:	*Inexpensive to moderate.*
RESTRICTIONS:	*Children discouraged. No pets.*

H oward Creek Ranch might well be described as a bed and breakfast resort. (It has a wood-fired hot tub, a sauna, and a pool set into the side of a mountain, forming a cabana with decks and a massage room.) Yet it also has many characteristics of an inn as well. The ranchhouse is 110 years old, and it has been restored with taste and imagination. The view is as picturesque as any you'll see — located amidst what was once a two-thousand-acre sheep ranch, the land is a vast panorama of mountains descending to grassy slopes that tumble abruptly into the sea.

It was in 1872 that Alfred Howard, newly arrived from Maine, built this ranchhouse. He and his family constructed two houses with the steeply pitched rooflines of the New England coast, and connected them in the middle as is typical in Maine. Thus was created a large, long structure with many bedrooms and lots of space. (One of the upstairs window panes has survived all these years intact, with the name of Lucy Howard — one of the original family members — scratched in the wave of the glass.) The residence was also used as a way station on a stagecoach line during its early years.

The house is built entirely from old-growth redwood and is set in a wide, secluded valley divided by Howard Creek; it faces the beach. (One can walk for miles here during low tide.) The house is filled with antiques, and the original fireplace still warms the parlor. There is something very secure and restful about Howard Creek's thick redwood walls.

Sunny Lasselle was a lighting technician in the film industry before he bought the Howard Creek Ranch in 1972; wife Sally had been traveling in South America, doing research for her degree in community development from Columbia. At first they opened their doors only to friends and people who had heard of them through word of mouth; slowly their home evolved into a bed and breakfast operation.

Breakfast is fresh fruit, muffins, juice, coffee, and tea. (Bacon and eggs are available on request.) Breakfast hours are flexible. Complimentary wine, beer, cheese, and crackers are served during the day and evening.

The rooms are generally spacious. They range in size, shape and atmosphere from a loft room in a redwood-paneled attic with a bed under a skylight, to a large and airy suite with an old iron bed and desk in one room and twin beds in another; the suite also has its own kitchen. As a very special extra Howard Creek has a music room with piano, organ, guitars, amplifiers and microphones, all for use by guests.

This area is just south of the Lost Coast, the last undeveloped wilderness area in California. Birds abound in these lovely environs; they include blue herons, hummingbirds, robins, kingfishers, and swallows who migrate to the ranch by the hundreds to build their nests in the barn (the largest on the Mendocino coast). Whales pass by here during winter and summer. In addition to wildlife, horses and cattle graze the fields. (Horses are available to guests who enjoy riding.) Westport Union Landing State Park is nearby, as is Abalone Park, a favorite spot for abalone gathering and rock climbing.

Howard Creek Ranch is an oasis in the wilderness — and it offers reduced rates for long stays as well as midweek and off-season accommodations.

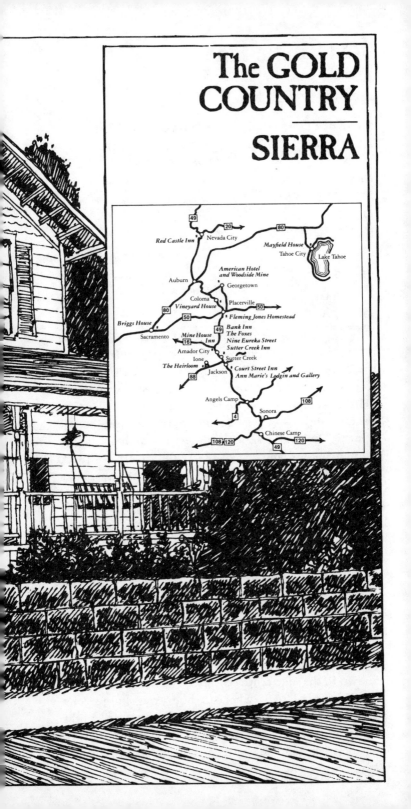

The GOLD COUNTRY

SIERRA

Red Castle Inn • Nevada City
49 20 80
Mayfield House • Tahoe City • Lake Tahoe
Auburn
American Hotel and Woodside Mine
Coloma • Georgetown
Vineyard House • Placerville 50
80
Briggs House • 50
Sacramento • Fleming Jones Homestead
49 Bank Inn
Mine House Inn The Foxes
16 Nine Eureka Street
Amador City • Sutter Creek Inn
Ione • Sutter Creek
The Heirloom • Court Street Inn
88 Jackson • Ann Marie's Lodgin and Gallery
Angels Camp
4 Sonora 108
Chinese Camp
108 120 120
49

Red Castle Inn

109 Prospect Street
Nevada City, California 95959; (916) 265-5135

INNKEEPERS:	*Chris Dickman and Jerry Ames.*
ACCOMMODATIONS:	*Eight rooms, six with private bath; double beds.*
RESERVATIONS:	*Two weeks recommended.*
MINIMUM STAY:	*Two nights over holidays.*
DEPOSIT:	*Full amount.*
CREDIT CARDS:	*Not accepted.*
RATES:	*Inexpensive to moderate.*
RESTRICTIONS:	*Children discouraged. Pets discouraged.*

Imposing is the word for this baronial structure high on Prospect Hill, overlooking the historic Gold Rush town of Nevada City. Four stories high, it is also one of the few classic examples of Gothic Revival — as opposed to the more popular Carpenter Gothic — to be found in the western states. (Gothic Revival was an architectural fashion in the United States from 1835 to 1880.) Built in 1859–1860, extensive gardens and a pond enhance the castlelike effect; a pathway on the grounds winds to the town below. Double brick walls make the interior considerably cooler on warm days, and add to the feeling of serenity and timelessness.

At 2,800 feet, Nevada City was one of the first towns set up by the forty-niners, who came from all parts of the world looking for the legendary quick strike in the Mother Lode (the Spanish called it the Veta Madre, and the name stuck). Some in fact did make their fortunes in gold; others prospered by furnishing the argonauts — the name by which the gold seekers were most frequently known in the nineteenth century — with basic goods and services. One man who did both was Judge John Williams. Crossing the plains in 1849, he stayed in the booming new city long enough to become a well-known businessman, a mine owner, a civic leader, and finally a judge. After two false starts he succeeded in erecting this monument to his industry. The Red Castle stands today as a reminder of the dreams of glory that motivated all who came to this near-wilderness and stayed to carve out a new state.

In 1963, James Schaar bought and restored the house; his wife managed it later as an inn. In 1978 it was bought by Jerry Ames, formerly a schoolteacher on the Monterey Peninsula, and Chris Dickman, a display coordinator for Macy's. They had seen an ad for the house in *Architectural Digest,* and just two weeks after taking possession opened their doors as a bed and breakfast inn.

The two proprietors have followed a middle course in furnishings. "We want it authentic, but also comfortable," Jerry comments. (The bathrooms retain the old-fashioned washbasins, but stall showers have been added.) The original pine floors and ceiling moldings are exactly as Judge Williams installed them; antiques of the period have been carefully selected for each room. Guest accommodations on the second floor are "parlor suites," each containing a small sitting area as well as a bedroom. Rooms on the first floor open up onto a veranda, and there is a tastefully appointed parlor, complete with old stereoscopic photographs and a viewer. A special extra is the theatrical masks collected by the owners from all points east, north, south, and west.

Breakfast is date-nut bread or muffins (both homemade), fresh fruit, and fresh-ground coffee. It is served buffet style between 7:30 and 11:30 A.M. Nearby attractions include plenty of gold mines, one of which is open for tours; also musical events, community theater, a bluegrass festival in neighboring Grass Valley, and a classical music event in June. Tahoe National Forest is nearby as well, and it is only thirty-eight miles to Soda Springs.

The *Smithsonian* calls the Red Castle a "perfect restoration," and the Daughters of the Golden West have acknowledged it as an important point of historical interest. It is a place where we come to revel in the gingerbread facade and icicle trim of another era's architectural imagination, but also to relax in the comfortable way its new owners have adapted it to the present.

Mayfield House

236 Grove Street
Tahoe City, California 95730; (916) 583-1001

INNKEEPER:	Joanne Neft.
ACCOMMODATIONS:	Six rooms with shared baths; twin, queen-, and king-size beds.
RESERVATIONS:	Two weeks recommended.
MINIMUM STAY:	None.
DEPOSIT:	First night's lodging.
CREDIT CARDS:	MC, VISA.
RATES:	Inexpensive to moderate.
RESTRICTIONS:	No children under twelve. No pets.

This reasonably priced and very special bed and breakfast began as the private residence of Norman Mayfield, who built it in 1932. The rooms reflect its history as a residence: Julia's Room commemorates Julia Morgan, a frequent visitor; the Mayfield Room, the builder himself; and the Den, the Study, and Mrs. Hinckle's Room are remembrances of the first principal of a local school who lived here while she pursued her teaching and administrative career.

Joanne Neft once owned and operated a travel agency, and initially envisioned the Mayfield House as an office. In the meantime she traveled as part of her job, and was consistently impressed with the way in which so many hotels seemed to overlook the little "extras" that make one's stay memorable (or even tolerable). The idea of using this warm and stylish home as a bed and breakfast seemed a good one, but at first Mr. Mayfield was not interested in selling. In late 1978 he changed his mind. Joanne took possession May 1, 1979, and opened June 27 — Mr. Mayfield's ninety-first birthday.

The furnishings are mostly original to the house. None are Victorian, but there are some striking Queen Anne and oak pieces, as well as some handsome Empire Revival ones. There is a large stone fireplace near which Joanne enjoys putting wood each night. There are no

telephones, radios, or televisions, but plenty of rare stonework, pleasant gardens, and beamed ceilings. All rooms have their own library; and down pillows, fresh flowers, and brass and copper accents are the rule. I also liked the original watercolors by Margaret Carpenter. (And the His and Hers velour robes — bravo, Joanne!)

This inn caters to both summer and winter activities — in fact its recreational proximity to skiing is one of the features that make it distinctive. Both cross-country skiing and golf are possible in season just across the street, and guests are within thirty minutes of seventeen downhill ski areas and twelve Nordic ski areas. In the summer guests are just a half block from Lake Tahoe and Commons Beach, as well as shops and restaurants; there is gambling at the state line.

Breakfast at the Mayfield House is Continental — and exquisite. Joanne tries to make something different every day. The day I was there that "something different" was Portuguese toast (sweet bread, pan-fried, with fresh fruit sauce), fresh mint from the garden, Danish Havarti cheese, fresh-squeezed orange juice, freshly ground coffee, tea, and milk. Joanne is also known for her apple strudel, sweet-potato muffins, and cheese blintzes with blueberry sauce. Guests can have breakfast in their rooms, on the terrace, in the breakfast room, or even in the homey living room. A newspaper accompanies each breakfast — a small but very accommodating extra.

American Hotel and Woodside Mine

Main and Orleans streets
Georgetown, California 95634; (916) 333-4499

INNKEEPERS:	*Al and Marion Podesta, Margie Whitelaw.*
ACCOMMODATIONS:	*Seven rooms, three with private bath; queen-size beds.*
RESERVATIONS:	*Two to three weeks recommended.*
MINIMUM STAY:	*Two nights.*
DEPOSIT:	*$10.*
CREDIT CARDS:	*Not accepted.*
RATES:	*Inexpensive to moderate.*
RESTRICTIONS:	*No children. No pets.*

Georgetown is one of those gold country villages that seem to exist in more than one time, the modern starkly accented by visible reminders of the Old West. Cars are parked along the main street — part of which still has the old wooden sidewalk — but it is not at all unusual to see a horse tethered in front of a saloon. It was once a place of quick (if not particularly easy) money, supported by the Woodside Mine once the gold panning became difficult. Directly behind the mine was built a spacious rooming house for miners, later a pleasure house with gambling and ladies of the night. Lola Montez, the legendary "spider dancer," once entertained here, according to local history.

The rooming house was also used as a way station by stagecoaches on the Wentworth Springs route to Tahoe. First finished in 1862, it suffered from at least three fires that razed the town during the 1880s, never quite succumbing but requiring partial renovation each time. In recent years it was a private residence and was allowed to decline.

Until it was bought by Al and Marion Podesta. She is German-born and came to this country when her industrialist father fled the Party bosses of East Germany for the freedom—and economic insecurity—of immigrant status in the United States.

Without a command of the language, Marion nevertheless succeeded at first as a model, later as a cocktail waitress. At the Timber Cove Inn at Jenner-by-the-Sea, she worked her way up to hotel manager. It was here that she met her husband Al, who was a part-owner of the Timber Cove Inn.

Restoration of the Woodside Mine turned out to be more difficult (and more lengthy) than Al and Marion could ever have predicted. Seven years later, the dream is coming true. The exterior has been painted ivory with Wedgewood blue trim, a redwood deck added for dining *al fresco*. Inside, the red fir floors have been stripped and refinished and a floor-to-ceiling rock fireplace built from native stone (the living room has twelve-foot ceilings). Four cramped rooms downstairs were turned into two; upstairs guest rooms have been furnished with wainscoting, crown moldings, and ornamental mopboards.

Breakfast is somewhere between full and Continental—but always a treat. Marion makes it a point never to serve any guest the same breakfast twice. The morning I was there I was privileged to receive excellent bagels (how I wish more inns would serve them), Colombian coffee, sweet butter, fresh fruit in season. Marion is also noted for her strawberry-filled German pancakes, and Westphalian ham or Canadian bacon, cut especially for her by her German butcher.

Guests may relax in either the breakfast room, with its bay window, Franklin stove, and French doors leading to the terrace, or the adjoining game room. Outside is Marion's aviary—birds are one of her passions—and her garden featuring a fine collection of bonsai trees.

Nearby attractions include Ponderosa Saloon (next door), twelve lakes "up country," and good fishing and gold panning. But this is essentially a place to get away from activities, not explore new ones. When asked about interesting going-ons in the area, Marion replied, "The Scotch broom blooms in April and May." She paused. "Just say that if you're feeling lost, Woodside Mine is a place where you can find a way back to yourself."

Vineyard House

Cold Springs Road off Highway 49
Coloma, California 95613; (916) 622-2217

INNKEEPERS:	*David Van Buskirk.*
ACCOMMODATIONS:	*Seven rooms, all with shared baths; twin, queen-, and king-size beds.*
RESERVATIONS:	*Two weeks recommended.*
MINIMUM STAY:	*None.*
DEPOSIT:	*Full amount.*
CREDIT CARDS:	*AE, MC, VISA.*
RATES:	*Inexpensive.*
RESTRICTIONS:	*No children. No pets.*

J anuary 4, 1848, was the day that changed the history of California forever — and the history of the United States. James W. Marshall was innocently supervising the building of a water-powered sawmill for his friend John Sutter, when some glittering specks of yellow caught his eye. "Boys," he said, "I believe I've found a gold mine." Since Coronado's time people had come to the New World in search of streets paved with gold, and this discovery fed perfectly into that aspect of the American dream. Within the next decade over 100,000 men would pour into the state seeking their fortunes.

Shortly after Marshall made his magic find in the American River, Coloma was a boom town of ten thousand people. Within ten years the magic had fled; prospectors moved on, following the Veta Madre to the north and south. One man who stayed was German immigrant Martin Allhoff. Like many another argonaut, Allhoff decided to quit the speculation (and danger) of mining and make money in more prosaic ways. He put his knowledge of wine making to use, starting a new vineyard that immediately attracted international attention for its over fifty varieties of wine (in 1872 he produced forty thousand gallons of wine and twelve thousand gallons of brandy).

Success was short-lived: he was soon to commit suicide over an alleged infraction of the law by a business associate. Robert Chalmers married Allhoff's widow and expanded the operations of the winery. He built this marvelous, rambling structure in 1878–1879, not only as a home for his family, but also as a hotel. A year later he was declared mentally incompetent, and his brother took over all his affairs. The hotel had one last moment of glory: in 1890 a huge ball was held to celebrate the dedication of a monument to James Marshall. Over four hundred persons were served at the first sitting for dinner, and Governor R. W. Waterman was in attendance.

The Herrera family, Vineyard House's modern owners, have performed marvels of restoration with this historic dwelling, yet have succeeded in keeping it a family operation. Still the visitor's first impression is that this is, first and foremost, a mansion. There are *five* separate dining rooms and four fireplaces on the main floor alone (all fires are kept lit during the winter months). There is a bar in the wine cellar, lined with stones cut by Chinese laborers in the 1840s; it features good live music on Friday and Saturday nights.

Upstairs are seven guest rooms, well furnished with antiques of the period. (Some rooms have brass bedsteads, others Victorian headboards; all have homemade quilts.) In the dining room I visited, kerosene lamps were in use, and downstairs there is a long and airy veranda, shaded by grapevines that were planted 110 years ago.

A Continental breakfast is currently served here: hot breads, coffee, and juice. Dinners are also served; unlike breakfast, they are not included in the price of one's lodging. Darlene Herrera is noted for her excellent desserts, which include chocolate cheese pie and walnut pie.

The Fleming Jones Homestead

3170 Newtown Road
Placerville, California 95667; (916) 626-5840

INNKEEPER:	*Janice Condit.*
ACCOMMODATIONS:	*Three rooms, one with private bath; double beds.*
RESERVATIONS:	*One week recommended.*
MINIMUM STAY:	*None.*
DEPOSIT:	*First night's lodging.*
CREDIT CARDS:	*Not accepted.*
RATES:	*Inexpensive.*
RESTRICTIONS:	*No children. No pets.*

T his delightful two-story, nineteenth-century farmhouse is the only bed and breakfast inn on the eastern side of the Sierra foothills of the Mother Lode. It's a good bet for those who seek total relaxation. No televisions, radios, not even a telephone — but there are ten acres to relax and ramble in. Since the Fleming Jones Homestead is also a working farm, eggs are for sale, there are chickens and burros, and stalls and pastures are available to those who enjoy giving their horses a vacation, too.

The Joneses were a pioneer family who settled in the area in the 1850s. Fleming Jones reputedly financed this home for his wife Florence with gambling money. She had wanted a new house for some time, when (according to family legend) Fleming came home late one night from a saloon where he was part owner. His cards had been lucky that night, and his pockets were full of money — which he promptly set down in front of his astonished wife. "There," he said. "Go build your house!"

Florence obeyed with alacrity. Something of an eccentric, she had her new dwelling built entirely of "clear" lumber — that is, planks without knots in them. (She was apparently of the belief that this would lessen the possibility of a residential fire, a great problem in those days.) The home was completed in 1883.

When Janice Condit began to renovate the old farmhouse, she asked Fleming Jones's granddaughter if she might use his name. The granddaughter was more than happy to give the venture her blessing. It's easy to see why — this is a respectful yet very comfortable venture into the homestead's past, one that respects its tradition as a working farm. (Janice lives in an old milk house that has been imaginatively converted into living quarters, adjacent to the main dwelling.)

The Lover's Fancy room is peach and white, with an old iron and brass bed. The Rose Room looks out onto a rose garden. The bed has a hand-carved high oak headboard; there is also an old-fashioned washbowl and pitcher. The Flower Basket room opens onto its own private balcony.

All rooms are decorated with country antiques. The parlor beckons with a corner rocker, where a variety of books and unusual periodicals, and sherry on the sideboard await your pleasure. Porches with swings and comfortable chairs overlook the homestead vegetable garden and adjoining meadows. Hikers can inspect the remains of mining equipment, mute testimony to the men who searched for gold here long ago.

Janice calls her breakfast "expanded Continental": homemade hot breads, rolls or muffins, farmhouse preserves, fruit breads, fresh fruit — including pears and apples from the orchard — sweet butter, and tea or fresh-ground French coffee. It is served at a massive table in the dining room that reminded me of the big tables at which my grandmother once fed my grandfather's threshing crews. If you've never had a grandmother with a farm in the country, a leisurely visit here will show you what you've missed — and once you've experienced that, you'll surely want more of the same.

Mine House Inn

South Highway 49
Amador City, California 95601; (209) 267-5900

INNKEEPER:	*Peter Daubenspeck III.*
ACCOMMODATIONS:	*Eight rooms, all with private bath; four double and four double twin beds.*
RESERVATIONS:	*Two weeks recommended.*
MINIMUM STAY:	*None.*
DEPOSIT:	*First night's lodging.*
CREDIT CARDS:	*Not accepted.*
RATES:	*Inexpensive.*
RESTRICTIONS:	*No pets.*

A mador means "love of gold" — and more than half the gold mined and gold panned during the boom years of the Gold Rush came from Amador County. It was here in Amador City that one of the first large gold quartz mining claims was staked out, in 1850. In 1851 the Keystone Consolidated Mine was formed, its total production eventually to exceed $24 million. The Mine House Inn is located in the old mine headquarters, a solid brick structure built in 1867, during the days when any mine headquarters was a likely target for bandits and highway robbers.

Peter Daunbenspeck had been in the hotel business in San Francisco for eleven years when he decided to manage the old Consolidated headquarters as an inn; the building itself had been in his family for almost three decades. It is the only inn in America made from such a structure. It is also one of the few bed and breakfast inns in the area that accepts children, a welcome accommodation for the traveling family. And it is the only one hereabouts that has a swimming pool for guests.

Peter has carefully furnished his inn with antiques that all come from the Mother Lode, within a hundred-mile radius of Mine House. The decor and ambience of the rooms make this place noteworthy.

The theme of each room is keyed to its original

function. In the Mill Grinding Room, for example, one finds the shaft supports still in the ceiling (these held the shafting used to drive the machinery for pulverizing the sample ore prior to assaying).

The Vault Room was actually once the huge safe in which all bullion was stored prior to shipping via Wells Fargo Stage to San Francisco. The Retort Room was where millions of dollars' worth of gold was smelted into gold bullion and carried by dumbwaiter to the vault. (The arch supporting this vault still remains.) The Stores Room with its warm red brick walls was where rock picks, tallow candles, and flasks of quicksilver were stored. The Directors' Room — with its high ceiling and private entrance to the front balcony — was where the affairs of the company were talked over, and profits were divided among mine owners and operators.

Orange juice, coffee, tea, and hot chocolate are available in the morning. The real attractions are the historical interest of the building, the reasonable rates, and the imaginative rendering of the rooms. It's also a good place for walking — Amador City has more than its share of historic buildings — and is centrally located for those who wish to explore some of the old mine sites. (In addition to Keystone Consolidated, the Plymouth Consolidated, the Central Eureka, the Kennedy, and the Argonaut mines are all within five miles of the Mine House Inn.)

The Foxes

77 Main Street
Sutter Creek, California 95685; (209) 267-5882

INNKEEPERS:	*Pete and Min Fox.*
ACCOMMODATIONS:	*One two-room suite;*
	queen-size bed.
RESERVATIONS:	*One week recommended.*
MINIMUM STAY:	*None.*
DEPOSIT:	*Full amount.*
CREDIT CARDS:	*AE, MC, VISA.*
RATES:	*Moderate.*
RESTRICTIONS:	*No children. No pets.*

T his is one of those places that remind one of the European bed and breakfast spots. But it's more than just a spare room; it is a very special luxury suite, intended to accommodate two people. Because it is private and intimate in atmosphere, it is called the Honeymoon Suite. (The proprietors — Pete and Min Fox — don't insist that their guests be honeymooners, but I can't think of a nicer place to spend one's honeymoon than in this intimately furnished little love nest.)

This charming two-story Victorian was once known locally as the Brinn House. It was built by Morris Brinn and his brother in 1857. Like so many who prospered during the Gold Rush, they sought their fortunes not in mines and gold pans, but in supplying the miners with the basic necessities of life in a gold camp: they owned a dry goods store in Sutter Creek, and a fairly large one at that. Their fine home has a definite New England flavor to it, typical of many of the old homes in this area and reflecting the origins of many of the settlers.

What is remarkable is that this quintessential Gold Rush Victorian was allowed to stand vacant for twenty-five years. In the 1960s it was rescued by a couple who began its restoration; later it was owned by another couple who continued the work and served lunch in a luncheon room in the building. The Foxes have now had it for two years, and the old Brinn residence has never looked better in its 125 years.

Their Honeymoon Suite consists of a sitting room, a bedroom, and a private bath. The bed has an amazing nine-foot-high headboard, and there is a matching marble-topped dresser (also nine feet tall) of walnut and walnut burl, circa 1875. The bedspread is a floral print coordinated with an antique floral-stripe wallpaper and the sheer drapes, which are tied back with a matching floral fabric. There is a Queen Anne love seat in the sitting room and another Queen Anne piece — a fine writing desk — that doubles as a breakfast table.

Breakfast at the Foxes is flexible. "Since there are only two people to consider," Min says, "we can talk about it once they get here." A typical breakfast might be fresh-squeezed orange juice, a very large fruit platter, sourdough French toast or blueberry muffins, and your choice of hot beverage.

Both Min and husband Pete come from Orange County. They got into the bed and breakfast business almost by accident. Pete had been in real estate for many years and envisioned the Brinn place as a possible office. The couple who were selling the house liked the Foxes' plan to open an antique shop there, but also spoke glowingly of the possibility of furnishing and renting the suite.

It was a natural. Min Fox well remembers her first customer. Jane Way of the neighboring Sutter Creek Inn called to say that a honeymoon couple had reserved the room, but in the bustle and rush of wedding arrangements had forgotten to mail their deposit. Could the Foxes put them up for a night? They could, and did. The next morning the bride and bridegroom watched the annual Italian Picnic Day parade from the Foxes' porch. "They got very emotional when they left," Min recalls. "And they came back for their first wedding anniversary. Since then we've become close friends."

There is nothing like a bed and breakfast inn to launch a new marriage — or to invigorate one that has been around a while. And there is no inn that I would recommend more highly for this than the Foxes'.

Sutter Creek Inn

75 Main Street
Sutter Creek, California 95685; (209) 267-5606

INNKEEPER:	*Jane Way.*
ACCOMMODATIONS:	*Seventeen rooms, all with private bath; twin, double, and queen-size beds.*
RESERVATIONS:	*Flexible, but phone as early as possible.*
MINIMUM STAY:	*Two days on weekends.*
DEPOSIT:	*$30 a day per room.*
CREDIT CARDS:	*Not accepted.*
RATES:	*Inexpensive to moderate.*
RESTRICTIONS:	*No children under fifteen. No pets.*

Huge lawns surround this deservedly well-known inn, and in summer garden furniture and hammocks are a delight under the redwood and laurel trees. An old and stately grape arbor is a haven for those who like to play cards during the day. Many fine restaurants are within walking distance of the inn and proprietor Jane Way keeps a book with guests' comments on local eating spots. Sutter Creek is itself a kind of living museum of architecture from 1860 to 1920. (If you wish to explore the town on foot, it is suggested that you pick up a copy of *Stroller's Guide to Sutter Creek* at the Tyler card shop on Main Street.)

Sutter Creek Inn was originally built as a Greek Revival by one of the town's leading businessmen, a man named Keyes, using redwood but following the style then current in New England. (It was a wedding gift to his homesick bride, a woman from New Hampshire.) It was owned later by State Senator Edward Voorheis, who married the Keyes's daughter in 1880. It was still in the possession of the same family when it was spotted by Jane Way, on a pleasure excursion through the gold country with her children. She fell in love with it instantly. After two months of calling daily, she convinced the family that she would be a worthy new owner of the historic building. "It's been well cared for," Jane says proudly, "and it's sturdy as a rock."

There is a large living room, with sherry on the sideboard. The color here is robin egg blue, and there are some Oriental pieces that go quite well with the country antiques. The large sofas are upholstered in floral prints, and I particularly liked the hutch with antique china and the grandfather clock. There is a very large library with current magazines and literally thousands of books, as well as a piano for the musical. Jane is a talented handwriting expert and will read your palm as well as your handwriting for character traits.

Jane is interested in psychic experiences — and it was perhaps because of that openness that she was once visited by a ghost. He was a distinguished-looking gentleman who said simply, "I will protect your inn!" and vanished. (Jane thinks he might have been Senator Voorheis.) Certainly he would be proud of her country kitchen, with its partially paneled brick walls, copper colanders, impressive collection of guns, and Oriental rug.

Many guest rooms are in what used to be outbuildings. Most have a distinctly country feeling, but are done with Jane's exquisite and quite sophisticated taste. Some rooms have patios; most have small libraries. Many have fireplaces, and one that I particularly liked contained a table made from a bass drum. Ceiling beams, canopy beds, and samplers are the rule in other rooms. Four of the rooms have beds suspended from the ceiling by chains and cables.

Jane likes variation in her breakfast menu, but a typical day's fare might consist of crispy fried potatoes with bacon and onions, sliced fresh fruit, buttermilk pancakes with raw apples and walnuts, and soft scrambled eggs with parsley.

At one time she stayed up each night to give guests a nightcap of brandy, but claims they kept her up too late. Now guests receive brandy in their morning coffee, if they so wish. If you *don't* wish, be sure to tell her, because Jane is as generous with her spirits as she is with her highly personable brand of vivacious hospitality.

The Bank Inn

6 Eureka Street
Sutter Creek, California 95685; (209) 267-0398

INNKEEPERS:	*Janelle Keith, Mimi Ford, Michael Ford.*
ACCOMMODATIONS:	*Five rooms, one with private bath; twin, double, and king-size beds.*
RESERVATIONS:	*Two weeks recommended.*
MINIMUM STAY:	*None.*
DEPOSIT:	*$25 a room per day.*
CREDIT CARDS:	*Not accepted.*
RATES:	*Inexpensive.*
RESTRICTIONS:	*None.*

Janelle Keith always wanted to own and manage a bed and breakfast. The Los Angeles native comes from a large family and likes having people around; she's also accustomed to cooking for large groups of family members at meals. A long time ago it occurred to her that she could make money doing essentially what she had been doing all along. The idea grew more attractive after she stayed at some bed and breakfasts on the East Coast. She had friends in Amador County, and with the help of her mother Mimi and her brother Michael, she went into business soon after buying this substantial Victorian dwelling.

No one knows exactly who built the inn, but it is known that it was erected in the late 1860s and was used as a boardinghouse for miners. (The mines around Sutter Creek were surprisingly long-lived; the main one closed down in the 1940s.) One room of the dwelling was used exclusively to store gold — one can readily imagine the security problems associated with *that* function. The house was owned until 1979 by an owner of one of the local gold mines, whose astonished heirs found $26,000 taped underneath a bureau.

"We'll be back," Janelle said when she first saw this house. "This is home!" And Janelle does run the Bank

Inn very much like a kind of extended-family dwelling. The coffeepot is always on; there are magazines and television in the common room. Children are welcome here — and pets — so it is tailor-made for the family on the move.

Brother Michael did most of the renovation work, with Janelle and Mimi adding attractive new wallpaper. Some four hundred plants have been planted, and Michael is working on a gazebo and a vegetable garden in the backyard. He also has high hopes for restoration of an old miner's shack on the banks of Sutter Creek; it may well end up as another guest room.

Breakfast at the Bank Inn is full, American, and *very* hearty. I was treated to a marvelous crustless quiche, a fresh fruit cup, orange juice, homemade bread and muffins, bacon (ham and sausage are also available), fresh eggs (collected from a friend who owns chickens), and coffee. In addition, Janelle's jellies, jams, and marmalades are all homemade.

There is a local legend that there is a bag of nuggets hidden somewhere on the premises of the Bank Inn, but no one has yet found it. Perhaps you will be the lucky one — although whether the nuggets would legally belong to the guest who found them is an open question. How about splitting it fifty-fifty, Janelle?

Nine Eureka Street

9 Eureka Street (P.O. Box 386)
Sutter Creek, California 95685; (209) 267-0342

INNKEEPERS:	*Gloria Jaggers and Marie Sanders.*
ACCOMMODATIONS:	*Five rooms, three with private bath; two twin and three queen-size beds.*
RESERVATIONS:	*Flexible.*
MINIMUM STAY:	*Two days on holiday weekends.*
DEPOSIT:	*$25.*
CREDIT CARDS:	*Not accepted.*
RATES:	*Inexpensive to moderate.*
RESTRICTIONS:	*No children. No pets.*

T he Lagomarsino clan were early settlers in the gold country, arriving in 1856. One of many industrious Italian-Americans who helped build up this area, Tobias Lagomarsino and certain other family members operated a stagecoach route on the Sutter Creek, Jackson, and Volcano line. It was not until 1916, however, that the family built this modest but very nice New England-flavored dwelling on two-block-long Eureka Street, just a block from Main Street.

The Lagomarsino home is now operated as a very comfortable bed and breakfast by Marie Sanders and Gloria Jaggers. The rooms are individually decorated in the mode of the past, but there is also air conditioning — not a minor consideration some summer evenings. The rooms are large, the atmosphere gracious; the tendency here is toward china and crystal, good silver, and linen napkins. Yet the ambience remains homey. I particularly liked the large porch, with its view of the surrounding hills.

Marie had been in the hotel business in San Francisco for three years when she heard that this California-style cottage was for sale. "And it was a *lot* of work," Marie acknowledges. But she has done very well, mixing English antiques with turn-of-the-century local ones. My favorite room is one that used to be a sleeping porch, featuring a beautiful carved bed; it has a light and airy feeling that is very restful.

The dining room sports chandeliers, leaded and stained glass windows, and elm wainscoting. The sitting room (which merges into the dining area) features beamed ceilings, plush carpets, and leather-covered stuffed furniture. The sitting room closes at 10:00 P.M., but until then the two proprietors invite you to "browse among the many books and revive the gentle art of conversation."

Breakfast is simple Continental fare: fresh orange juice, fruit compote, homemade muffins, coffee, tea, or milk.

Sutter Creek is centrally located in the gold country. There is excellent fishing at the well-stocked low-elevation lakes: Camanche, Pardee, and Amador. Fairs, rodeos, and local festivals are the rule in summer. Kirkwood Meadows, one of California's best ski areas, is not far away. Or you may simply wish to drive around the small roads leading away from Highway 49. From Main Street, drive up Sutter Hill Road past the abandoned Botto Saloon and the Central Eureka Mine, or along Amador Road, past the Union-Lincoln mine site. These and other byways leading from Sutter Creek are lined with ancient stone walls and occasional crumbling stone buildings from the Mother Lode's colorful past.

Court Street Inn

215 Court Street
Jackson, California 95642; (209) 223-0416

INNKEEPER:	*Mildred Burns.*
ACCOMMODATIONS:	*Five rooms, three with private bath; twin, double, and queen-size beds.*
RESERVATIONS:	*Two weeks recommended.*
MINIMUM STAY:	*None.*
DEPOSIT:	*First night's lodging.*
CREDIT CARDS:	*Not accepted.*
RATES:	*Inexpensive to moderate.*
RESTRICTIONS:	*No children. No pets.*

T he main part of this house was built in 1870 for the Isaac Peiser family, on what was then called Corral Hill. (Apparently the area was used for grazing cattle in those early days.) Only three years later Mr. Peiser and his young son died, victims of diphtheria. The remainder of the wealthy merchant's family continued to live here until the house was sold to the Blairs, who owned the Jackson Water Works, and their daughter Grace Depue.

The Miwok Indians were frequently unable to pay their water bills in cash, so they made payments in the form of baskets and other artifacts. Grace Depue kept her collection in a brick house in the back; in her will she donated it to Stanford, and at the time of her death it was appraised at $90,000. In this way a priceless collection of Miwok folk art was preserved for the enjoyment of all Californians.

Mildred Burns had visited the gold country frequently from her home in San Luis Obispo, vacationing at bed and breakfast inns. She was looking for a way to make a living, and to take care of aging parents at the same time. The present dwelling seemed to have everything: it was a home of the Victorian era, with a small house in back for her parents. Restoration began in May

1980; the first guests arrived before work was even finished, in April 1981.

That first week a woman called from San Francisco. She wanted to be married in Jackson — could she have three rooms for the wedding party? "And that was on only two days' notice," Mildred points out. "Before it was over I ended up finding a minister for them, and we had the wedding right here in the parlor. *And* the reception." It was Mildred's blunt introduction to a certain fact of life: the proprietor of a bed and breakfast inn often ends up being a social secretary.

My favorite room at Court Street is the Peiser Room. It has its own sun porch, a sitting area with wicker pieces, old quilts, and fresh flowers, and some fine Queen Anne furniture; the colors here are bright green and white. (There are also ruffled pillow shams and a pitcher and washbowl.)

There are Oriental pieces throughout the house: rugs, ginger jars, and, in the larger parlor, a lovely lacquered Chinese screen. (Mildred explains that these kinds of pieces — particularly Chinese screens — were widely used during Victorian days.)

Despite what Mildred calls the "Early American Gold Rush" ambience of her carefully designed and decorated rooms, all of them are air-conditioned. Complimentary wine or tea is served in the guest rooms, sherry in the parlor. A full breakfast is served at Court Street Inn: French toast, granola, strawberries and yogurt, homemade breads (including pumpkin-banana nut), egg dishes, crêpes and quiches, orange juice, and tea or coffee. All are made especially enjoyable by the friendly company of your hostess and proprietor, a unique woman who combines vivacity with character — an admirable compound that seems especially appropriate to this very magical part of California.

Ann Marie's Lodgin and Gallery

410 Stasel Street
Jackson, California 95642; (209) 223-1452

INNKEEPER:	Ann Marie Joseph.
ACCOMMODATIONS:	Three rooms, all with private bath; twin and double beds.
RESERVATIONS:	One to two months recommended.
MINIMUM STAY:	None.
DEPOSIT:	First night's lodging.
CREDIT CARDS:	Not accepted.
RATES:	Moderate.
RESTRICTIONS:	No pets.

Ann Marie Joseph was raising her children alone, working two jobs for very little money; yet she was a frustrated writer and painter. Her dilemma was the ancient struggle between the needs of the creative artist and the more prosaic needs of society at large. How could she realize her creative ambitions and still make enough money to feed her children (and herself) in this area of somewhat limited employment and business opportunity? She decided that a bed and breakfast was the answer, and got herself a job with another local inn to see how the business end worked.

"I saw a lot of families being turned away because they had children," Ann Marie says; and since she is a mother, she naturally finds herself sympathetic to those with "little folks." So it should be no surprise that she encourages families. It is not unusual for large families to book more than one room, and Ann Marie will babysit infants and young children for a very reasonable $3 an hour.

Built in 1892, this Victorian was used by Dr. James Wilson both as a personal residence and as an office for his patients, most of whom were miners and their families. Ann Marie has furnished it throughout with country pieces, most of which belonged to her parents or her Portuguese grandparents. The parlor and sitting room contain her quilts and handsewn stitchery, as well as a wood-burning stove; out back there is a garden swing for the young and the young at heart.

Rooms are named after their original functions in Ann Marie's residence. Mama's Room is my favorite: an antique brass bed, lace curtains, a private bath with a claw-foot tub, and an old-fashioned beveled, mirrored bird's-eye maple dresser all add to the atmosphere of quiet country leisure. There is also an antique trunk that belonged to her grandparents, who brought it with them around the Cape on their long passage to the New World.

One unusual and very pleasing aspect of this inn is the original art on the walls. Many of the paintings are Ann Marie's. ("And people actually buy 'em," she remarks cheerily.) Works of Sutter Creek artist Joan Tarr and local copper handcrafter Gerry Raddatz are also displayed.

Ann Marie's Continental breakfast usually features linguisa meat pie, fruits in season, juice, and coffee with brandy. In the evening guests receive complimentary iced tea or wine; hot toddies are served in the winter. As of this writing, Ann Marie was serving large dinners on Sunday nights for $10.

Ann Marie says, "I have the best of both worlds now, the world of work and the world of creativity." Which is not surprising, as this energetic and youthful woman is blessed with talent in both areas.

The Heirloom

214 Shakeley Lane
Ione, California 95640; (209) 274-4468

INNKEEPERS:	*Patricia Cross and Melisande Hubbs.*
ACCOMMODATIONS:	*Four rooms, one with private bath; twin, double, queen-, and king-size beds.*
RESERVATIONS:	*Two to three weeks recommended.*
MINIMUM STAY:	*None.*
DEPOSIT:	*First night's lodging.*
CREDIT CARDS:	*Not accepted.*
RATES:	*Inexpensive to moderate.*
RESTRICTIONS:	*No pets.*

Part of California's fascination is due to the diversity of its people. This is reflected in its variety of architectural styles — particularly in the gold country, where people from many parts of the country converged at once. A good example of this is the Heirloom, a bed and breakfast inn in Ione. Obviously built by a Southerner, this two-story brick Colonial mansion with an antebellum arch replicates perfectly the prevailing fashion in the South before the Civil War.

Built in 1863 by a Virginian (who also built another Southern-style mansion in Ione), the structure was soon purchased by Dr. Luther Brusi, who in 1870 was a veteran of the Confederacy. He must have felt very much at home in this lovely dream house, with its stately columns, verandas, and white-wood balconies. Somewhat later it was sold to James and Catherine Browning (Catherine remained here until 1923); James was associated with the famous Browning rifle company.

The house was bought by Patricia Cross and Melisande Hubbs in 1980. Both had been looking around Sonoma and Carmel for a dwelling appropriate for a bed and breakfast, when they heard of this place. Ione is somewhat off the tourist track; it was never a boom town, but a supply center for the mining camps. Yet when they saw this undeniably breathtaking structure they knew it was the right one for them.

All windows are deep-set in the Southern style. (The house and garden are completely hidden from public view by shrubs and trees.) The front entrance boasts a fan transom. The living room is completely paneled in wood painted off-white, as was the custom in early days. The high ceiling and paneled windows (draped in gold brocade), stained pine floor with area rugs, Colonial staircase and mantel are an elegant background to the antique furnishings in this very livable mansion.

Pat and Melisande are quite flexible toward guests; one is not encumbered with a surfeit of rules and regulations here. "I like to see the tension melt out of people's faces, after they've been in the country a while," says Melisande. One of the pieces they are most proud of is their grand piano, once the possession of Lola Montez, famed "Gold Rush queen" of Grass Valley. This instrument has an offset keyboard and heavy, beautifully carved rosewood legs.

The rooms are named for the seasons. The Winter Room has a fireplace; burgundy and pale-blue tones predominate. The Spring Room, in yellow and green, has lovely handmade quilts, an old-fashioned rocker, and gay white wicker furniture. The Autumn Room has a brass bed, a comforter, and pillow shams with matching duet ruffles. The Summer Room features pink rose wallpaper, cool green and beige tones, and a quilt on the wall; it also contains an old trunk that came to California in a covered wagon, and a very nice Queen Anne desk.

Sherry, white wine, or tea is served in the early evening, and guests find fresh flowers, fruit, and candy in their rooms. Breakfast is full — and very generous. On a typical morning you will receive fresh-squeezed orange juice, crêpes with fresh fruit topping, popovers and croissants, cheese (Brie), and gourmet coffee from Louisiana. In keeping with the Southern theme, Pat and Melisande usually serve food while wearing long aprons and skirts, adding to the sense of calm and antebellum luxury that is so much a part of the Heirloom.

The Briggs House

2209 Capitol Avenue
Sacramento, California 95816; (916) 441-3214

INNKEEPERS:	Bob and Sue Garmston, Barbara Stoltz, Kathy Yeates, Paula Rawles, Penny and Craig Carolan.
ACCOMMODATIONS:	Five rooms, two with private bath; twin, double, and queen-size bed.
RESERVATIONS:	Three to four weeks recommended.
MINIMUM STAY:	None.
DEPOSIT:	$20.
CREDIT CARDS:	VISA.
RATES:	Inexpensive to moderate.
RESTRICTIONS:	No children. No pets.

Doctor William Briggs was born in Ohio and after studying his eye, ear, nose, and throat specialty in Europe, he settled and began his practice in Sacramento. The Capital City was still something of a frontier town in those days. Technically not itself within the Gold Country, it, along with San Francisco, was one of the two centers of civilization toward which the weary miners turned when they were ready to spend their hard-won *noveaus riches*. So we should not be particularly surprised that Dr. Briggs was the first U.S. medical man to report the "removal of steel from an eye with a magnet," as written by one of his contemporaries. Life was hard in the mining towns, and in the cities it was sometimes brutal and capricious.

But already the Gold Country was slowly turning from mining to more dependable pursuits, among them the lumber business and the embryonic tourism industry. The two are not always compatible callings: Dr. Briggs was one of the original organizers of the Save the Redwoods League, bitterly opposed by the lumber interests. At the same time he was becoming something of a civic leader, a friend of those in high places. In 1901, he bought this cube-type Colonial Revival (Neo-Federalist, if one wishes to be really specific about architectural styles) dwelling, shortly after it was built, and continued to live here until his death in 1931.

What luck, then, that this quintet of lively and imaginative women (and two husbands) got together to restore and manage it as an inn. At this writing, it is the only bed and breakfast inn in Sacramento. All the partners are in the same occupation (education), all nonetheless have different approaches to decorating, yet somehow managed to make the interiors compatible — despite the fact that each partner decorated a separate room.

The Heritage Suite has a queen-size bed and floor-length tieback drapes in blue, with accessories of the period (lace pillows, perfume bottles, linens, and an old dress hanging on the wall). My favorite was the Sunrise Room, which features a private balcony with white wicker rocker and table which catch the morning sun. It has baby blue walls, armoire, an antique hand-carved double bed, comforter and pillows in beige lace, and a plush carpeted bath.

Guests at the Briggs House are met with linen-lined baskets of fresh fruit and almonds, and wine is brought to the room in the afternoon (or mineral water, according to one's taste). Guests are encouraged to enjoy the large front porch, with its comfortable porch swing. In addition there are the common areas where guests may relax and mingle, if they wish: a well-stocked library, sitting room (once the home's dining room) and backyard garden — a very pleasant place with its picnic table, fig and plum trees, framed by redwood latices. Bicycles are available. (Sutters Fort, the Capital buildings, Railroad Museum, Old Town, and the Crocker Art Museum are all nearby.)

The
CENTRAL
COAST

1

17

Santa Cruz

Watsonville

101

Castroville

1

Salinas

Pacific Grove
Gosby House
Green Gables
Old Monterey Inn

68

101

Carmel

Monterey

Holiday House
Sea View Inn
Stonehouse Guest Lodge

1

Big Sur

San Luis Obispo
Heritage Inn

Green Gables

104 Fifth Street
Pacific Grove, California 93950; (408) 375-2095

INNKEEPERS:	*Roger and Sally Post.*
ACCOMMODATIONS:	*Three rooms, all with shared bath; twin and double beds. Accommodations available June through August only.*
RESERVATIONS:	*Six to eight weeks recommended.*
MINIMUM STAY:	*None.*
DEPOSIT:	*Full amount.*
CREDIT CARDS:	*Not accepted.*
RATES:	*Moderate.*
RESTRICTIONS:	*No pets.*

William Lacey, of the prominent Monterey Laceys, created this Queen Anne-style mansion in 1888, literally by the water's edge. A Judge Wilbur used it as a summer home in the 1890s; in this century the Gerrard family was responsible for the intelligent and systematic improvements that have kept Green Gables in mint condition. Always an impressive residence, with its wide-angle view of Monterey Bay, this relatively small but elegant dwelling has been an inn since 1958.

Roger and Sally Post were living in Pasadena when they first stayed here on a visit to the area. They told their astonished hosts that they would like nothing more than to buy it; and sure enough, when it was finally put on the market, it was to the Posts that the owners first turned. "It was one of those things that just happens," Sally says. "Call it luck — or providence."

They add that Pacific Grove has many of the advantages of a small town, but isn't isolated: the Monterey Peninsula has all the activities and attractions of any large metropolitan area. Shopping, tennis courts, boutiques, golf courses, bike paths, swimming, and the world-famous 17-Mile Drive are all close; many are within walking distance. (Rooms are available at Green Gables

only during the summer months, however, and the Posts book a great deal of repeat business — so call early.)

The living room features cozy blue crumpled-velvet love seats by a fireplace, a gay carousel horse, and silk flowers. There is a pool table downstairs; in the formal dining room there is a panoramic view of the coastal shoreline. Here also there is a fireplace, and several fine Oriental rugs. Family photos grace the stairway.

The Garret Room has a gabled roof, floral wallpaper, and an iron bed with comforters; an appealing little hideaway, this. The Balcony Room has a delightful closed-in balcony with a stupendous view of the ocean. The Gable Room contains twin beds, a large desk, and blue and white wallpaper; both beds have old quilts and red bedspreads, a cheery bit of contrast that I liked.

The breakfast is Continental: homemade bread, bagels, croissants, juice, and coffee or tea served in the dining room from 7:30 to 9:30. There are fine gourmet restaurants situated in other historic homes in Pacific Grove; the Posts are more than happy to help with reservations and directions.

The Gosby House

643 Lighthouse Avenue
Pacific Grove, California 93950; (408) 375-1287

INNKEEPERS:	*Roger and Sally Post.*
ACCOMMODATIONS:	*Nineteen rooms, thirteen with private bath; double and queen-size beds.*
RESERVATIONS:	*Two weeks for weekdays, five weeks for weekends.*
MINIMUM STAY:	*Two nights on weekends.*
DEPOSIT:	*Full amount.*
CREDIT CARDS:	*Not accepted.*
RATES:	*Moderate.*
RESTRICTIONS:	*No pets.*

The Gosby House Inn, which like Green Gables is owned by Roger and Sally Post, is one of those fascinating places that have been inns right from their inception. The founder of this inn was one J. F. Gosby, an industrious native of Nova Scotia who made his way to the sunnier climes of California in 1853. He had learned the shoemaking trade at an early age and soon became the town's only cobbler. In the meantime he kept his eyes open for the main chance — which came in 1875, when the Methodist Church established religious conference grounds in a secluded area near the ocean. The shrewd Gosby, a Methodist himself, decided that an inn was needed to house the visitors and participants in the many religious and cultural activities that took place there.

So in 1887 Gosby built this comfortable, rambling inn and began almost immediately renting rooms to visitors attending the various meetings sponsored by the church. (His inn, in addition to being near the grounds, was also right across the street from the Methodist Church.) Gosby was civic-minded, gregarious, a member of many lodges, and a Town Council member from 1892 to 1896. Meanwhile the Southern Pacific railroad extended their tracks to Monterey and built the beautiful

Del Monte Hotel, also during the 1880s (building the smaller El Carmelo Hotel to handle the overflow). This brought even more visitors.

Just as the area had become firmly established as the place of choice for vacations and religious retreats, the Del Monte burned to the ground. The demand for accommodations was now overwhelming; Gosby's fortunes soared. He added a round corner tower and bay windows (late 1890s), as well as electric wiring, indoor plumbing, and connecting doors (early 1900s). In the 1920s the irrepressible cobbler changed the name of his inn to the El Carmelo Hotel, no doubt to take advantage of the more famous caravansary's name.

From 1930 onward the inn changed hands several times, finally being purchased by the present owners in 1976. It has now been rehabilitated in a manner that reflects its original glory, and is once again called by its original name. Fresh paint, brass fixtures, marble sinks, and antique furnishings throughout reflect the over twelve thousand hours necessary for restoration.

Look for the rare doll collection in the entry parlor when you arrive (and the old photograph of Mr. Gosby in front of his shoe shop). There are fresh flowers and fruit in all rooms, and complimentary sherry in the afternoon. But the real distinction of the Gosby is in the many extras that one does not often find in a bed and breakfast. Shoes left outside your door are shined by the "Boots" (shades of an English inn); you have your choice of newspapers with breakfast, including the *Wall Street Journal* (for those who can't seem to make the total break from the financial/business world). A hall porter will arrange theater tickets and dinner reservations. Bicycles are available for riding along the Pacific Grove shoreline. (Watch for migrating gray whales from December to March, plus sea otters, pelicans, and other shore birds.) An English taxicab is available to take you to places around town.

Breakfast here is Continental. Special services at the Gosby include an iron and ironing board, a sewing kit, alarm clocks, and a very thoughtful policy of celebrating special occasions such as birthdays, weddings, and anniversaries.

Old Monterey Inn

500 Martin Street
Monterey, California 93940; (408) 375-8284

INNKEEPERS:	*Ann and Gene Swett.*
ACCOMMODATIONS:	*Nine rooms, five with private bath; twin, queen, and king-size beds.*
RESERVATIONS:	*Two to three months for weekends.*
MINIMUM STAY:	*Two nights on weekends.*
DEPOSIT:	*First and last night's lodging.*
CREDIT CARDS:	*Not accepted.*
RATES:	*Expensive.*
RESTRICTIONS:	*No children. No pets.*

No doubt about it, this place is special. The only word that works here is *elegance*. And what a pleasure it is — particularly because the elegance is achieved without a hint of the ostentatious! Located in a quiet area near the heart of Monterey, the inn is surrounded by lovely gardens that create the illusion of an English country house. Architecturally it is in fact English Tudor, and owners Ann and Gene Swett have given it many of the characteristics of the finest English (and Scottish) inns.

The dwelling was built in 1929 by Carmel Martin, a former mayor and civic leader of Monterey. (It is now included in the National Registry of Historic Homes.) After passing through several hands, it was bought and restored by the Swetts. Used exclusively as a private residence until the last of their six children flew the nest, a visit to the Sutter Creek Inn caused the Swetts to consider the possibility of creating a country-style bed and breakfast inn in the heart of Monterey. They have most definitely succeeded — to the lasting delight of the hostelry's many regular guests, including visitors to the world-famous Monterey Jazz Festival.

Typical of the careful architectural detail to look for at this inn are the huge timber beams and posts in the vestibule. Hand-carved designs on the stairs were done by August Gay, an artist in the community who is also responsible for the window valances.

Besides its sensational setting, it was the extras that won me over at the Old Monterey Inn. The beds aren't just beds — they're experiments in total luxury. There are soft *and* firm pillows for each guest, and European goose down comforters. Free soft drinks and juices are stored in a refrigerator on the second floor. Breakfast is served on fine china. In the bathroom medicine cabinet I discovered the following: shampoo, nail polish remover, toothpaste, a hair dryer, a curling iron, and electric curlers. Rose petals from the garden are used to make potpourri that guests may take with them as gifts.

Branches from an old oak frame an enchanting view from the window of the Garden View room. Guests in the Library Room enjoy both a sun deck and a fireplace in this book-lined hideaway that was once actually a library. Visitors in the Dovecote room can relax by a fireplace in shadows cast by a skylight. Shades of the Orient make the Eastwinds a special experience; The Cottage features a sitting room with stained glass. (The Cottage also has a cozy seat in the bedroom bay window with a view of the garden.)

Breakfast here is Continental, but generous — and very good. The day I was there the following was available: fresh fruit, orange juice, cheese rolls, croissants and whole-wheat muffins as well as coffee, tea, and Sanka. Scones, fruit compotes, brioches, and toast with ollalieberry jam are also served some mornings (this jam is homemade, and a specialty of the area). Those who wish to remain in their rooms may have their morning meal served on a tray, in bed if they wish. On pleasant mornings breakfast is served on a terrace. (For couples who desire privacy there are secluded tables in the garden.) Complimentary wine and cheese is served every afternoon at 5:00.

The Swetts are firm believers in a quote from Boswell's *Life of Johnson:* "There is nothing which has yet been contrived by man by which so much happiness is produced as by a good tavern or inn." This is one of those rare places that delivers total serenity and pleasure.

Sea View Inn

Camino Real between Eleventh and Twelfth
Carmel, California 93921; (408) 624-8778

INNKEEPERS:	*Marshall and Diane Hydorn.*
ACCOMMODATIONS:	*Eight rooms, six with private bath; twin, queen- and king-size beds.*
RESERVATIONS:	*Three weeks recommended.*
MINIMUM STAY:	*Two nights on holidays and weekends.*
DEPOSIT:	*First night's lodging.*
CREDIT CARDS:	*MC, VISA.*
RATES:	*Inexpensive.*
RESTRICTIONS:	*No children under eight. No pets.*

Here's another economical bed and breakfast where one can park the car and take it from there on foot. (It's three blocks from the beach, five from Ocean Avenue, Carmel's main street.) This country-style Victorian, built in 1906, is one of the oldest guest houses in this artists'-colony-by-the-sea. Yet it is well out of the tourist crush; located in a residential neighborhood, there is no traffic noise or other distractions associated with congested downtown areas.

The Sea View is popular as a honeymoon haven; don't be surprised if you meet guests returning for their anniversaries. (One couple who had spent their wedding night here fifty years ago returned recently on their fiftieth anniversary.) It is also patronized regularly by visitors to the jazz and Bach festivals, both annual events in Monterey and Carmel, respectively. (Book a room early if you are attending either; accommodations are hard to get during the festivals.)

Proprietors Marshall and Diane Hydorn first visited Carmel looking for a vacation house. (Marshall was flying for TWA and Diane was occupied as a homemaker, raising the couple's children.) More as a joke than anything else, they asked the real estate agent if there were any "little inns" for sale. "As a matter of fact, there is one," was the sobering reply. The Hydorns were hooked as soon as they saw it.

This is an adult hideaway where privacy is everything, but children over eight are allowed as long as they are reasonably well behaved. The Sea View is furnished with antiques blended in with newer pieces; a great many belongings of the hosts are to be found around the house, too, adding to the personal feeling of the inn. Both Hydorns try to give their guests as much attention as possible. (There is a full selection of games, and the Hydorns are well informed about local happenings and attractions, including good local restaurants.)

The Continental breakfast is served in the living room, before the fireplace, and varies from day to day. When I visited there were assorted cold cereals, juice, fresh fruit, whole-grain toast, and muffins. (And, of course, a choice of hot drinks: tea, coffee, herb tea, and cocoa.) A tasty coffee cake is served other mornings, and on certain Sundays Diane has been known to make quiche as a special treat. Complimentary sherry is served in the afternoon.

Holiday House

Camino Real and Seventh
Carmel, California 93921; (408) 624-6267

INNKEEPERS:	*Kenneth and Janet Weston.*
ACCOMMODATIONS:	*Six rooms, two with private bath; twin, double, and king-size beds.*
RESERVATIONS:	*Eight weeks for weekends.*
MINIMUM STAY:	*Two nights on weekends.*
DEPOSIT:	*First night's lodging.*
CREDIT CARDS:	*Not accepted.*
RATES:	*Inexpensive.*
RESTRICTIONS:	*No infants. No pets.*

Kenneth and Janet Weston were living in Palo Alto when they first visited the Monterey Peninsula. (Ken was a school administrator; both were looking for something different.) The place they stayed happened to be a country-style inn whose owner was also a real estate agent. They told him of their dream of owning an inn of their own. He found this handsome cottage for them almost immediately. "We came as guests of an inn," Janet observes, "and woke up owners."

The brown-shingled dwelling was built in 1905 by a Stanford University professor as a family summer home — and also as a retreat for students and faculty. The living room and sun porch (both of which are open to guests) have a marvelous ocean view, a stone fireplace, books, games, and a grand piano. There are also gardens for guests to enjoy: all of the six bedrooms look out to sea, or onto a garden. The house is perfectly located; it's a five minutes' walk to the beach or to village shops, galleries, and a wide variety of restaurants.

Holiday House has been furnished with antiques and collectibles, most purchased locally. There is no TV or swimming pool here; the Westons feel that such conveniences defeat the objective of a bed and breakfast inn, which is rest and relaxation. There is a small pond on the grounds, with a terrace and a stone bench, which adds to the introspective mood of the place. Not that it is without whimsey: all rooms have fresh flowers — but are also stocked with a full supply of jellybeans! (Rooms that share a bath also have washbasins, a very country touch.) Some rooms are directly under the sloping roof, which imparts a cozy, hidden-away feeling.

Most rooms are furnished in decor appropriate to the turn of the century; some of the art work is original, by local artists (ask Kenneth and Janet which ones they are — they just might be for sale). Extras include plush towels and luxurious bed linens.

The Point Lobos room features a fine view of Point Lobos and has *both* queen and single beds. Rustic paneling, decorative shades, and blue, red, and beige patterns in both wallpaper and bedspread set an upbeat mood. The Jenny Lind room has a fine brass bed, chairs with needlepoint, and an eye-catching green Laura Ashley print.

Breakfast is served buffet style between 8:30 and 9:15, in the living room or on the sun porch (or one can take it to one's room). There is a selection of cold cereals, hot bread, coffee cake, rolls, fresh fruit, and English muffins.

Since Holiday House has been a guest house since the 1920s, staying here has become a family tradition with some guests. Its pronounced order and cleanliness, its relaxing atmosphere, and its reasonable rates all make it a real find — particularly for those who must watch their budgets, but still wish to avoid the impersonality of the big hotels and faceless motels that have proliferated in the area.

Stonehouse Inn

Monte Verde and Eighth
Carmel, California 93921; (408) 624-4569

INNKEEPERS:	*Roger and Sally Post.*
ACCOMMODATIONS:	*Six rooms, all with shared bath; double and king-size beds.*
RESERVATIONS:	*Four to six weeks for weekends.*
MINIMUM STAY:	*None.*
DEPOSIT:	*Full amount.*
CREDIT CARDS:	*Not accepted.*
RATES:	*Moderate.*
RESTRICTIONS:	*No children under twelve. No pets.*

Stonehouse was built in 1906 by Josephine Foster, Carmel's resident bohemian. She was a great friend of the arts — of writers particularly — and among her guests were the brightest literary lights of her time: Jack London, Sinclair Lewis, Mary Austin, poet George Sterling. (In those days one didn't have to write, drink, or throw wild parties to be considered bohemian — all one had to do was be a patron of the arts.) Josephine was known affectionately as "Nana" by her friends, of whom there were many on the Monterey Peninsula.

Nana's family was artistic. Her grandfather had built the first Cliff House in San Francisco (destroyed later by fire). Stonehouse reflects her idiosyncratic taste. All the stones are carefully arranged and mortared together in the manner of the stone houses of Pennsylvania; creeping vines cover its exterior. Records show that the stones were hand shaped by local Indian craftsmen, and the unique star-shaped window in the front of the dwelling may have been fashioned by one of these men.

Stonehouse is furnished with country-flavored antiques throughout. The living room features a large stone fireplace (sherry and hot cider are served to guests here before they leave for dinner in the evenings). All guest rooms have handmade quilts, silk flower arrange-

ments, fluffy pillows, and complimentary fresh fruit.

The rooms are named after authors. One named after George Sterling (it was he who wrote that San Francisco was a "cool grey city of love") contains a handsome king-size canopy bed, a dressing screen, a white eyelet comforter, a dust ruffle, pillow shams, and old pictures on the wall; also featured are an antique dresser and a comfortable rocking chair and reading lamp for quiet moments with a book. The Jack London room has an antique armoire and a queen-size bed with a wrought-iron and brass frame. (It also has a couch that can fold down into another bed.) Both rooms have good views of Point Lobos.

My favorite room was the Sinclair Lewis. Large and airy, with a huge brass bed, this room's big windows overlooking the rooftop and trees reminded me of the rooms at grandmother's house when I was a very small child.

The Continental breakfast varies from morning to morning, but is fairly generous. Croissants, bagels, juice, homemade bread, and pastries are served from 8:30 to 10:00 A.M., and guests may eat either in the dining room, or — in good weather — on the patio.

One interesting legend about Stonehouse: Nana Foster is reputed to have placed "important papers" within the stone walls on the left-hand side of the fireplace. Writings by her accomplished literary friends? Some of her own literary efforts, perhaps? We may never know. "No one's been able to tear the fireplace apart to find out," says manager Joseph Smith. "The fireplace is too beautiful."

Heritage Inn

978 Olive Street
San Luis Obispo, California 93401; (805) 544-7440

INNKEEPERS:	*Rob and Kathy Strong.*
ACCOMMODATIONS:	*Eight rooms, one with shared bath; seven double and one queen-size bed.*
RESERVATIONS:	*Three weeks recommended.*
MINIMUM STAY:	*None.*
DEPOSIT:	*First night's lodging.*
CREDIT CARDS:	*MC, VISA.*
RATES:	*Inexpensive.*
RESTRICTIONS:	*No children. No pets.*

T he history of the Heritage Inn in San Luis Obispo sounds more like the Perils of Pauline than the usual guidebook fare. The saga began in 1902, when the San Luis Obispo Herrera family (one of the old Hispanic families in the area) built this gracious three-thousand-square-foot home as a family dwelling. As its ten bedrooms would indicate, the Herreras were a large family: Manuel was the city's constable, Isbaldo the custodian at the courthouse; Juanita, the oldest daughter, worked for the Tribune Printing Company. About 1930 the residence was sold to Frank Barcellos, a local saloon owner who moved it around the corner to Santa Rosa Street and used it as a lodging establishment for men.

In January 1981 the building was bought by Rob and Kathy Strong, who hoped to renovate it and use it as a bed and breakfast inn. ("It was not a totally rational decision," Kathy recalls. "We indulged in a little romanticism and idealism — but who doesn't at some time?") The condition of the sale was that the Strongs move the structure to another location to make way for a parking lot. The couple scheduled the house's dramatic half-mile move, only to be halted at the last moment by a neighboring motel's protest. Some frantic legal maneuvering followed — capped by the court's decision that the Heritage Inn could be moved, just hours before the wrecker's ball would have demolished it forever.

An interesting sidelight: the inn's new location was bought from another branch of the Herrera family. And where was this new creekside location for Heritage Inn? Right where it started out, back in 1902!

I'm glad the good guys won this round, because this is not just the only bed and breakfast in San Luis Obispo; it is a quality establishment by any standard, run by a caring and capable couple who have the right combination of good taste and solid business savvy to make this a howling success.

The character of the inn is turn of the century: antique furnishings (most from the area), stained glass, period wall coverings and draperies, bay windows and window seats throughout, period bath fixtures, and a wide and well-chosen variety of San Luis Obispo memorabilia and photos. Guest rooms are provided with brass, wicker, and oak antiques; quilts; abundant fresh flowers; and washbasins.

The reception room provides a large variety of local tourist information and a menu selection from local restaurants. (The Heritage management is quite eager to help — and there is a resident manager on call all night, a very civilized touch.) Parking is easy, and there is little traffic noise in this old residential section of the city. Wine and cheese are served in the parlor in the evening; bubble bath is available in the bathrooms, as is unusual soap (including mint and chocolate!). Bikes and picnic lunches can be provided to guests in an exploring mood.

The Continental breakfast is served buffet style in the fireside dining room: croissants or bagels, homemade spreads, juice, coffee, or tea. A local baker comes in every day to make the pastries — just one of the reasons people from San Francisco, Los Angeles, and the San Joaquin Valley are finding Heritage Inn the ideal mid-coast stop during that long drive down El Camino Real.

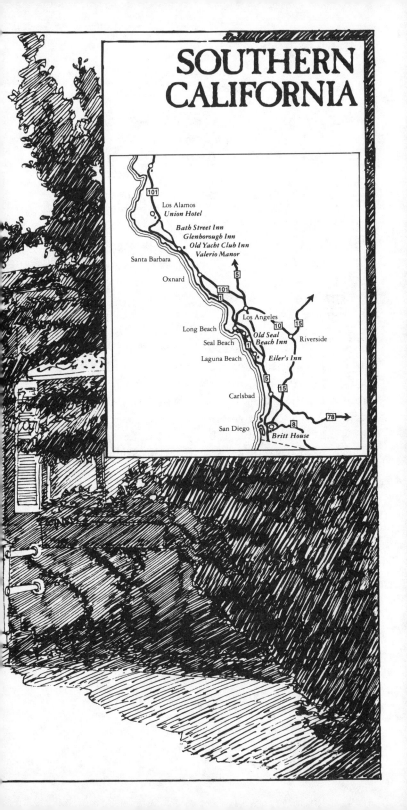

SOUTHERN CALIFORNIA

Los Alamos
Union Hotel

Bath Street Inn
Glenborough Inn
Old Yacht Club Inn
Valerio Manor

Santa Barbara

Oxnard

Los Angeles

Long Beach

Seal Beach
Old Seal Beach Inn

Riverside

Laguna Beach
Eiler's Inn

Carlsbad

San Diego
Britt House

Union Hotel

362 Bell Street
Los Alamos, California 93440; (805) 344-2744

INNKEEPERS:	*Kathleen Johnson, Dick and Teri Langdon.*
ACCOMMODATIONS:	*Twelve rooms, two with private bath; one twin and eleven double beds.*
RESERVATIONS:	*Three to six weeks recommended.*
MINIMUM STAY:	*None.*
DEPOSIT:	*First night's lodging.*
CREDIT CARDS:	*Not accepted.*
RATES:	*Moderate.*
RESTRICTIONS:	*No children. No pets.*

J. D. Snyder was a New Yorker who came west to make his fortune — and succeeded. In the 1880s he owned the way station in tiny Los Alamos for the stagecoach route between Santa Barbara and San Francisco. In addition to being the local agent for Wells Fargo, he was also involved in farming and a variety of other business ventures in Santa Barbara County. One of them was the Union Hotel, where stage passengers could eat, stay overnight, and wet their whistles before continuing the arduous overland journey.

Fire destroyed the hotel, however, as it did so many other wooden structures of that time. In 1915 it was rebuilt with Indian adobe. Thereafter it was used as a hotel, a rooming house, and a pool room, after which it was boarded up and forgotten. Until it was discovered by Dick Langdon, that is. It became his dream to rehabilitate — or recreate — this old western hotel based on original sketches of the Union. Wood from twelve barns was used to recreate the exterior; various craftspeople in the area contributed their talents. The result is a work of art that has attracted comment from western buffs and bed and breakfast enthusiasts alike.

Antiques here are imaginative and provocative: two-hundred-year-old Egyptian urns; a pair of swinging doors from a New Orleans house of ill repute; dining room furniture from a Mississippi plantation; an 1880 Brunswick pool table.

My room was a masterpiece of whimsey: a ceiling fan, an antique trunk, and hats hanging from a coatrack! (I kept waiting for the owners of those hats to come back and claim them.) In the evenings Dick likes to play tapes from his collection of old radio shows. There is an evening meal — children are charged by their weight. There is an old crank telephone, and guests who listen carefully to the earphone are often surprised by mysterious (taped) voices.

One of the most interesting architectural and designing triumphs of this inn is the swimming pool. There were no such conveniences in the 1880s, so Dick concealed this one in the guise of an old-fashioned reflecting pool. The grounds also include streetlights, park benches, flower gardens, and manicured lawns. There is a lovely Victorian gazebo with a secret Jacuzzi underneath (raised hydraulically at night), large enough to accommodate a dozen guests.

A full breakfast is served, and it is as special as everything else about the place. It has been known to include such diverse fare as gingerbread cake, chocolate chip cookies, pound cake, and brandy. After breakfast guests are treated to a tour of Los Alamos in a 1918, fifteen-passenger touring car.

This distinctive adventure in lodging is only open on Friday, Saturday, and Sunday (all year round). "Three days a week is fun," Dick is often quoted as saying. "After that, it becomes work." Be sure to book early — word of mouth has made the Union Hotel one of the most popular attractions in the area.

The Old Yacht Club Inn

431 Corona Del Mar
Santa Barbara, California 93103; (805) 962-1277

INNKEEPER:	*Nancy Donaldson.*
ACCOMMODATIONS:	*Four rooms, all with shared bath; queen-size beds.*
RESERVATIONS:	*Three weeks for mid-week; three months for weekends.*
MINIMUM STAY:	*Two nights on weekends.*
DEPOSIT:	*First night's lodging.*
CREDIT CARDS:	*Not accepted.*
RATES:	*Moderate.*
RESTRICTIONS:	*No small children. No pets.*

T ake four independent career women. Add a historic structure crying out for tender loving care. Stir in a need to try something new and different, and you have the highly successful ingredients of one of Santa Barbara's newer and most comfortable bed and breakfast inns.

The Old Yacht Club Inn was built in 1912 as a private residence on Cabrillo Boulevard overlooking the beautiful Pacific. In the 1920s Santa Barbara's yacht club was completely destroyed by a disastrous storm. The present structure was pressed into service as the head-quarters for the club; later it was moved to its current location on Corona Del Mar.

Nancy Donaldson, the dean of a Los Angeles high school (she is currently on leave), and three female friends — also educators and administrators — coop-erated to buy, renovate, furnish, and finally operate the Old Yacht Club Inn. Just a short distance from lovely Cabrillo Beach, the OYCI has four tastefully decorated guest rooms.

Although all share baths, rooms come with wash-basins; there is a small decanter at bedside for guests whose slumber is improved by a sip or two of sherry. The two front rooms have balconies surrounded by flowers. The Castellamare room is my favorite: hardwood floors, a window seat, bedspread and drapes with a brightly colored flower print. (I also liked the Portofino room, with its baby blues and tan and cream.) All rooms are decorated with antiques, and the front rooms catch the sun and a delicious afternoon breeze.

Guests are invited to share the living room area as well as the spacious front porch. (Arriving guests are given a glass of wine or a cup of tea in the living room.) There is a fireplace here, but no TV. As a native of the area, Nancy is well equipped to steer guests to the best restaurants and nearby attractions. Bicycles are available to guests, as are beach chairs and towels. Guests who arrive on Amtrak or at the airport can be picked up.

The Continental breakfast is fuller than most, usually featuring egg dishes, with fresh fruit, juice, homemade breads (zucchini and banana), and coffee cake. Nancy will also cook dinner for guests who request it in advance. Request it — she's an *excellent* cook!

Valerio Manor

111 West Valerio Street
Santa Barbara, California 93101; (805) 682-3199

INNKEEPERS:	*Joy Simon and Rebecca Wamsley.*
ACCOMMODATIONS:	*Five rooms, one with private bath; twin and queen-size beds.*
RESERVATIONS:	*Four weeks for weekends.*
MINIMUM STAY:	*None.*
DEPOSIT:	*First night's lodging.*
CREDIT CARDS:	*Not accepted.*
RATES:	*Moderate.*
RESTRICTIONS:	*No children. No pets.*

T his Federal-style Colonial was built in 1904 as the Blanchard-Gamble Boarding School for Girls, a finishing school dedicated to what was then deemed the proper upbringing of Santa Barbara's young ladies. Later, in 1914, it served as the boarding department of the Santa Barbara Girls' School. Continuing the tradition of female ownership and residence, Valerio Manor became a sorority house in the 1950s. The insignia of a local fraternity, etched into the window of the Simonette room, endures as a reminder of the pledge parties and the ubiquitous panty raids of the period.

Joy Simon had been visiting bed and breakfast inns in the San Francisco Bay Area for years; her position as a real estate salesperson made it relatively easy to look for the property that would help her realize her dream of owning one herself. She joined with Rebecca Wamsley in the purchase of Valerio Manor, and the two women work together in its day-to-day management. (As artist in residence, Rebecca will be happy to tell you which of the works of local artists featured at the inn are for sale.)

Valerio Manor greets the arriving guest with a fireplace-warmed parlor, with a piano; there is also a garden room and a dining area, both graced with Joy's needlework and silk flowers. The spacious grounds invite you to stroll, lounge, or play croquet. The central location puts restaurants, theaters, the art museum, and the historic courthouse all within walking distance. (A telephone is available to guests.)

The Southwest Room — the quietest of the five — was my favorite. (Early California with a Hopi Indian rug and a Gorman print.) This room, with its earth tones of brown and rust, also has a fireplace and a very comfortable queen-size bed. The Simonette is named for the tiny-floral-print wallpaper; this cheery room is accented with original watercolor paintings and a Monet print.

The Green Room is a genteel, sun-washed affair with a deep forest-green wall and bed coverings and botanical prints. Also sunny, with a wood parquet floor, Oriental rug, and rattan furniture, the Camellia Room is located downstairs, with a fireplace and a private bath. And for American country at its best, there is the large Master Room with a fireplace, old rose wallpaper, and needlepoint chairs.

The Continental breakfast is usually fresh-squeezed orange juice in chilled glasses, croissants, muffins (blueberry the day I visited), and a unique blend of coffee, Dutch chocolate, and cinnamon. The morning meal is at 9:00 and can be taken in the dining area, garden room, in one's own guest room, or — on nice days — in the garden.

Bath Street Inn

1720 Bath Street
Santa Barbara, California 93101; (805) 682-9680

INNKEEPERS:	*Susan Brown and Nancy Stover.*
ACCOMMODATIONS:	*Five rooms, two with private bath; twin, double, queen-, and king-size beds.*
RESERVATIONS:	*Six weeks recommended.*
MINIMUM STAY:	*Two nights.*
DEPOSIT:	*Two night's lodging.*
CREDIT CARDS:	*Not accepted.*
RATES:	*Moderate.*
RESTRICTIONS:	*No children. No pets.*

From the time Vizcaíno entered the harbor on the eve of Saint Barbara's Day in 1602 (and so, appropriately, named the channel for her), Santa Barbara has been a magnet for adventurers, visionaries, entrepreneurs, and most of all people irresistibly attracted to its mild climate and scenic beauty. Both newcomers and old Santa Barbara hands have found the Bath Street Inn ideally located for maximum enjoyment of the city's rich cultural and resort activities.

Bath Street Inn began as a private residence in 1895, and was called the House of the Three Sisters by local residents. (At least partly because of the huge *Pittosporum* tree with three trunks that stood outside, it would seem.) When Susan Brown found it with the aid of a realtor, the old dwelling was badly in need of some sisterly attention. And it got it — with the help of a local architect who did much of the renovation.

A common theme among owners of bed and breakfast inns is a desire to leave an environment of cutthroat ambition and enter a service-oriented world. Susan — a personnel manager in Anaheim for ten years — was no exception. This charming and intelligent woman pronounced herself "somewhat disillusioned with the business world." Or at least its most competitive and least reflective aspects.

At the same time, she offers services that businesses of all descriptions find eminently helpful: seminar facilities and a conference room. There is also an outdoor barbecue, and Susan plans to install a Jacuzzi.

This Queen Anne Victorian has three stories with a small second-story eyelid balcony in front, and is larger inside than it appears from the street. (The third floor — where the common area is located — feels like an entire house in itself.) The rooms are decorated with a nice mix of antiques that combine the 1895 atmosphere of the original dwelling.

The Continental breakfast is served outdoors on the porch or patio when weather permits — which it usually does in Santa Barbara. It consists of homemade breads, rolls, coffee cake or croissants, juice, fresh fruit in season, and a choice of coffee, tea, milk, or cocoa.

The Glenborough Inn

1327 Bath Street
Santa Barbara, California 93101; (805) 966-0589

INNKEEPERS:	*Jo Ann Bell and Pat Hardy.*
ACCOMMODATIONS:	*Four rooms, all with shared bath; two double and two queen-size beds.*
RESERVATIONS:	*Two to three months for weekends.*
MINIMUM STAY:	*Two nights on weekends.*
DEPOSIT:	*Full amount.*
CREDIT CARDS:	*MC, VISA.*
RATES:	*Moderate.*
RESTRICTIONS:	*Children discouraged. Pets discouraged.*

T he Glenborough is a handsome, two-story structure built in 1906 in what is often termed the California Craftsman style. Built by a single craftsman for Louis Brooks, vice president of a local fuel company, it was quite modern for its time, with a decorative brass heater instead of the traditional wood fireplace. But in renovating, decoration and design has mainly followed the turn-of-the-century mode of the architecture. With few exceptions, furnishings are antiques — even the curtains are of old lace, crocheted, and there is even one pair of knitted curtains. Rooms have pictures from the early 1900s, and a very special part of the decor are the original nineteenth-century watercolors on loan from a local gallery.

Proprietors Jo Ann Bell and Pat Hardy met when they served together on the board of directors of a battered women's shelter in Riverside. Jo Ann has a background in social work as a psychotherapist, and still maintains a small practice. Pat is a former director of a crisis hotline, a people-oriented bundle of creative energy whom Jo Ann describes as a "greeter, a morning person, and a risk-taker." The decorating was done mainly by Pat, with Jo Ann "keeping things from getting outrageous."

The French Rose room is graced by elegant inlaid French furniture and a rose velvet spread; my favorite of all four rooms in the main house, this spacious chamber has a fine mountain view framed by antique embroidered curtains. Aurelia's Fancy celebrates a young woman who once lived here, with a rocking chair, a full queen-size cannonball field bed accented with rich blue, antique lace curtains and an heirloom quilt. The Country room projects a cozy ambience, its earthy tones enlivened by the morning sun, with antique golden oak furniture. The Garden room is the smallest but cheeriest, a former sun porch overlooking a garden, with an antique brass and white iron double bed; furniture is wicker and antique oak, accented by lush plants.

Wine and tea are served in a pleasant parlor in the evening; there is a hot tub in the garden that may be reserved. On chilly nights guests can request an old-fashioned footwarmer to be tucked between the sheets, and most beds have four fluffy pillows. Pat and Jo Ann have just opened four new rooms in an early 1880s cottage across the street, with separate entrances, a secluded New Orleans-style garden, and a private bath for each room.

Breakfast at the Glenborough was delicious. A platter of fresh fruit (baked apple in wintertime); homemade coffee cake and nut breads (pumpkin and banana); orange, cranberry, or apple juice; and tea, cinnamon-laced coffee, or cocoa. The morning meal is served between 8:00 and 9:30, and is served to guests in their rooms — in bed if desired.

"We don't necessarily emphasize a homey atmosphere that much," says Pat. "We believe many of our guests come here for privacy."

The Old Seal Beach Inn

212 Fifth Street
Seal Beach, California 90740; (213) 430-3915

INNKEEPERS:	*Marjorie and Jack Bettenhausen.*
ACCOMMODATIONS:	*Twenty-two rooms, all with private bath; twin, double, queen, and king-size beds.*
RESERVATIONS:	*Two weeks recommended.*
MINIMUM STAY:	*Two nights on weekends.*
DEPOSIT:	*First night's lodging.*
CREDIT CARDS:	*AE, MC, VISA.*
RATES:	*Inexpensive to moderate.*
RESTRICTIONS:	*Children discouraged. No pets.*

T he Spanish called it Rancho Los Alamitos; the German burghers who followed knew it as Anaheim Landing. Bay City was the rather slick monicker cooked up by developers in the 1920s. Today this sleepy coastal village is known as Seal Beach (after the many seals that once flocked to the beaches here), but it is in many ways just as quiet now as it was in former days — which for those of us who wish to get away from it all is a big plus. Yet the nearby convergence of three major freeways make Los Angeles and destinations in Orange County easy to get to when it's time to get back to the real world.

The style of the Old Seal Beach Inn is French Mediterranean, a perfect choice for this part of the state. When one first hears of its twenty-two rooms, one imagines that this might be a motel that serves breakfast. Not a bit of it! The rooms are equipped with antiques and warm, quality furnishings, carefully designed to impart a Continental country inn flavor. (All rooms have private baths, and kitchen-bars are available in most units.) Prints, objets d'art, collectibles, and books abound in most rooms. There is a pool, as one might expect in southern California; and there is also an attractive garden with roses, geraniums, hibiscus, and begonias (among other flowers).

Seal Beach Inn began as a motel in the 1920s, when Seal Beach was a wide-open gambling and resort area, which makes the European feeling of this place all the more remarkable. ("The closest thing to Europe since I left there," reads one encomium in the register.) Hardwood floors and wood paneling are everywhere. Antique lamp posts and a brick courtyard, blue awnings and a yellow-painted fence, and an ancient British telephone booth all add to the ambience.

Proprietors Marjorie Bettenhausen and physician husband Jack go out of their way to provide those little extras that make a bed and breakfast different from any other kind of accommodation. Current magazines and the *Los Angeles Times* are available in the breakfast room; there are laundry facilities for the use of guests (including an ironing board). Just one block from the ocean, Seal Beach Inn is also close to the Old Town section of Seal Beach (the high percentage of artists and craftspeople living in the area is obvious in the boutiques and shops), the Long Beach marina, and a total of four shopping areas on various waterfronts. (And the inn is just fifteen to twenty minutes by car from the *Queen Mary*, Knott's Berry Farm, and Disneyland.)

Breakfast in the breakfast room begins at 8:00 and lasts until 9:30. French and American pastries, marmalade and butter, freshly squeezed OJ, and coffee and tea are all served buffet style — although one can have them brought to the room on request.

Marjorie and Jack enjoy what they do, as becomes obvious when one talks to them about their work. "Every day it's something different," Marjorie told me. One interesting moment came when two attractive French girls admitted sadly that they had run out of money. What to do? Before a call could be placed to the French Embassy, two French pilots checked in, and *voila!* . . . the next day the two young women were flown back to Paris free of charge. A charming story, and one that might have an interesting follow-up . . .

Eiler's Inn

741 South Coast Highway
Laguna Beach, California 92651; (714) 494-3004

INNKEEPERS:	*Jonna Iversen and Kay Trepp.*
ACCOMMODATIONS:	*Twelve rooms, all with private bath; twin, double, queen-, and king-size beds.*
RESERVATIONS:	*Four to five weeks recommended.*
MINIMUM STAY:	*Two nights on weekends.*
DEPOSIT:	*First night's lodging.*
CREDIT CARDS:	*MC, VISA.*
RATES:	*Moderate to expensive.*
RESTRICTIONS:	*Children discouraged. No pets.*

Eiler Larsen was a Danish immigrant with a passion for wishing people well — an agreeable eccentricity (if eccentricity it really is) that made him a well-loved local figure in Laguna Beach. The colorful Dane simply loved to say hello to people, and each day strode up and down Laguna Beach greeting residents and strangers alike. In the 1960s he was made the town's official greeter by the municipal government, and as the irrepressible old gentleman grew older and declined in health, the tabs for his meals and lodging were quietly picked up by government and business people. When he passed away in 1975, he left a warm memory of a man who represented perhaps the highest form of hospitality: a desire to make others feel good with no reward for oneself except the company of one's friends.

Oddly enough, Jonna Iversen was born in the same place as Eiler: the town of Aarhum, Denmark. She also was attracted not only to the New World but to the southern California part of it; she owned a boutique in Laguna for several years. Together with Kay Trepp (who has an art and design background), she purchased what was to become Eiler's Inn, a gentle reminder of her kindly countryman and the friendliness he brought to their new home in America.

Eiler's Inn is a small establishment, despite its

twelve rooms, arranged around a marvelous fountain courtyard that is definitely more Hispanic than Scandinavian. Cheese and a fruit board greet the newly arrived guest, as do complimentary champagne or sparkling cider. (Afternoon tea is also served around the courtyard fountain.) There is often live music during the wine hour on Saturdays. Both Jonna and Kay are well acquainted with the area and are happy to recommend local eating and entertainment spots.

There is a fireplace in the parlor, and a library is generously stocked with games and puzzles; there is also an attractive sun deck on the second floor. Rooms are decorated with a southern California 1940s motif (the premises began as a hotel in the early 1940s): vintage TV's, rose-patterned rugs, and speckled linoleum floors look as though they might have been part of a film set for *Chinatown* — if there had been a bed and breakfast inn as comfortable as this one in the film of that name. (All rooms have a private bath.)

The buffet-style breakfast is served in the courtyard between 8:30 and 10:30. It includes fresh fruit in a seashell, tomato or orange juice, hard-cooked eggs, pastries, and freshly ground coffee. The courtyard at Eiler's Inn is one of the most pleasant places imaginable to begin one's day, and in the bright smiles and good company of Jonna and Kay one is assured that the tradition of friendliness personified by Eiler Larsen is very much alive.

Britt House

406 Maple Street
San Diego, California 92103; (714) 234-2926

INNKEEPERS:	*Daun Martin and Robert Hostick.*
ACCOMMODATIONS:	*Nine rooms, one with private bath; one double and eight queen-size beds.*
RESERVATIONS:	*One week for weekdays, six months for weekends.*
MINIMUM STAY:	*Two nights on weekends.*
DEPOSIT:	*First night's lodging.*
CREDIT CARDS:	*MC, VISA.*
RATES:	*Moderate to Expensive.*
RESTRICTIONS:	*Children discouraged. No pets.*

I t is not only San Diego's only bed and break-fast inn (at the time this was written), but one of the best anywhere. "From Mendocino to the stormy coast of Maine," raves the *LA Times,* "it is with-out a doubt the most perfectly restored Victorian serving America's travelers today." Such tributes by a large met-ropolitan newspaper do not come every day; and when one visits this romantic gabled and turreted Queen Anne delight, one begins to understand what the shouting is all about.

Set in a neighborhood experiencing an extensive renovation of Victorians, Britt House was built in 1887 for Eugene Britt, an attorney active in civic and state affairs. (It was later owned by the Scripps family, famous in newspaper publishing circles.) It was discovered by Daun Martin and Robert Hostick, who together sank over $100,000 into restoring the proud old mansion. One of its most impressive — and justly famous — fea-tures is a stained-glass window two stories high, backing a winding staircase. Screens of wooden beads grace the doorways; hardwood floors and old wood paneling are used with the utmost imagination and taste. (Robert's excellent line drawings also appear in various places around the house.)

The furnishings in the guest rooms enhance the romantic mood. The Governor's Room overlooks a garden, and its blue and white color scheme is enhanced by the personal furniture of Governor Robert Waterman, the state's seventeenth governor. King Ludvig's Room contains an ornately carved couch and headboard that once belonged to "mad" King Ludvig of Bavaria. The Island View Room is done in caramel, cream, and burgundy; one can see the ocean while sitting at its gateleg table, and its braided rug, carpet-backed reclining rocker, and Eastlake dresser add to the sense of luxury. Fresh fruit and candy kisses are available in all rooms, and one bath has a sauna.

Breakfast is Continental, and imaginative. On Sundays, for example, Robert fixes his famous dish of fresh fruit smothered in whipped cream flavored with Grand Marnier, Mexican vanilla, orange zest, and nutmeg — with a strawberry on top. Yeast bread is made the night before and allowed to rise overnight. Viennese roast coffee is ground on the premises and prepared filter-drip style. There is sweet butter and jam for the homemade bread. There are also hard-cooked eggs and a choice of tea or coffee.

Bed and Breakfast
Referral Services

Following is a list of agencies that book reservations and refer travelers to bed and breakfast inns as well as accommodations in private homes. These services are gaining in popularity, and the rooms in private homes include breakfast as well as overnight lodging at very affordable rates (costs range from $12–$45 per night).

Operations vary. Some services charge the traveler an annual membership fee, while others take their commissions from the host providing the lodging. In some cases the agencies provide lists or directories of the homes they contract with and leave the arrangements up to you.

San Francisco Bed and Breakfast Club USA
110 Tiburon Boulevard, No. 5
Mill Valley, CA 94941
Provides quarterly guide to b&b accommodations in private homes; annual membership $35.

San Francisco Private Room Service   (415) 931-3083
2185-A Union Street
San Francisco, CA 94123
Homes in San Francisco and Marin County; rates from $35–$45 per night.

Bed and Breakfast International   (415) 525-4569
151 Ardmore Road
Kensington, CA 94707
Referral service. Accommodations in California homes; rates from $19–35 per night.

The Bed and Breakfast League   (609) 921-0440
20 Nassau Street
Princeton, NJ 89540
Homes in fifteen U.S. cities including Los Angeles, San Diego, and San Francisco; $45 membership fee; room rates $12–28 per night.

The International Spareroom   (714) 755-3194
Box 518
Solana Beach, CA 92075
Provides list of in-home accommodations available in California for $1; room rates range from $12−$35 per night.

Rent-A-Room International   (714) 640-2330
1032 Sea Lane
Corona Del Mar, CA 92625
Homes in southern California; $15−$25 per night.

Home Suite Homes   (408) 733-7215
1470 Firebird Way
Sunnyvale, CA 94087
Homes providing bed and breakfast throughout the United States and overseas; $20 membership fee; room rates $16−$25 single, $25−$45 double.

Bed and Breakfast Santa Barbara   (805) 684-3524
4744 Third Street
Carpinteria, CA 93103
Central Coast referrals; room rates $25 single, $30 double.

Digs West   (714) 739-1669
8191 Crowley Circle
Buena Park, CA 90621
Reservation service for bed and breakfast homes in southern California; rates $18 single, to $42 double.

Northwest Bed and Breakfast   (503) 246-8366
7707 Southwest Locust Street
Tigard, OR 97223
Western states referrals; annual membership fee $15 single, $20 family. Room rates $14−$21 single, $18−$30 double, $26−$34 family.

California Bed and Breakfast
P.O. Box 1551
Sacramento, CA 95807
Referral service. Annual membership $15; rooms $15−$30 per night.

Wine Country Exchange   (707) 963-7127
P.O. Box 88
St. Helena, CA
Bed and breakfast referral service for Napa and Sonoma counties; $5 each booking.

Visitor's Advisory Service   (415) 521-9366
1516 Oak Street, No. 27
Alameda, CA 94501
Short-term bed and breakfast home accommodations in the San Francisco Bay Area.

B.B. International
1318 Southwest Troy Street
Portland, OR 97219
Has contract arrangement with AMTRAK to provide bed and breakfast accommodations for AMTRAK passengers; available only through travel agents.

Other bed and breakfast publications of interest to Californians and California-bound travelers:

Bed and Breakfast American Style $6.95.
   by Norman T. Simpson
Berkshire Traveller Press
Stockbridge, MA

A National Guide To Guest Homes $4.95.
   by Maxine Coplin
220 Redwood Highway, No. 113
Mill Valley, CA 94941

Bed and Breakfast Homes Directory $6.50.
10938 Northshore Square
Cupertino, CA 95014
Northern California listings.

Guide To Guest Houses and Tourist Homes USA
   by Betty R. Rundback
P.O. Box 335-A
Greentown, PA 18426

Northern California Inns
   Toby Smith, Publisher
P.O. Box 3383
Santa Rosa, CA 95402
Newsletter; reviews of bed and breakfast and country inns in northern California. $20 annually.

Index